Subscription Box
BASICS

Subscription Box

BASICS

**A 30 DAY PLAN TO GET
YOUR BOX IDEA OFF THE GROUND**

by **JULIE BALL**

*Founder of Sparkle Hustle Grow
+ Subscription Box Bootcamp*

ISBN: 978-1-948604-88-8 (Paperback)
ISBN: 978-1-948604-95-6 (Ebook)

Library of Congress Control Number: 2020915262

Published by Kat Biggie Press
Columbia, SC
www.katbiggiepress.com

Cover Design by Carmen Vermillion
Interior Design by Fresh Design
Edited by Dakota Nyght

Table of Contents

Gratitude 1

Introduction - A note from Julie 3

1. What's your why? 9
2. What's so great about subscription boxes? 29
3. How does the subscription box model work? 39
4. Getting started 49
5. The lingo 59
6. Carve out your concept 67
7. Be the solution 85
8. Competitive research 99
9. How to make a profit 107
10. Product sourcing 117
11. Brand packaging 131
12. Operational life cycle 139
13. Pre-launch steps 145
14. Common launch mistakes 161
15. Commit 167

Resourcres 178

About the Author 179

Sending Gratitude

As with everything in my business, I could not do it without the help of my amazing support system. From family to friends to colleagues and you.

Special shout outs to my husband Kenny and daughter McKenna, my parents, my in-laws, family and friends. The support you provide is unwavering and I'm lucky to have you all in my corner. I'm usually the cheerleader, but it's so nice to have cheerleaders of my own.

Big thanks to…

The Sparkle Hustle Grow and Subscription Box
Bootcamp leadership team:
Renae, Amy, Carmen, and Hilary.
Love you ladies!

My Subscription Box Mastermind Sisters:
Jessica, Abby and Betsy.

Subscription Box Bootcampers

Sparkle Hustle Grow subscribers aka Sparklers

Alexa Bigwarfe and her squad
at Kat Biggie Press Publishing

Introduction

A Note From Julie

I know you. You are ambitious, but feeling stuck. You're so ready to finally launch your subscription box without the overwhelm. You want to help others through your box business, and you don't want someone else to beat you to it. So, day after day, you head to Google for more searching...

You've researched for weeks and joined five new subscription box Facebook groups in the past few days. The excitement you felt about launching your subscription box is now stuck in the decision paralysis of moving parts. Tech, products, profit margins... SERIOUSLY!? You're losing all motivation to move forward with your subscription box idea.

You've read blogs, watched a bunch of videos, and now you feel more confused than ever, trying to piece together how to do sourcing, box design, and marketing on your own. Then you head down the software rabbit hole. It might be a while before your family sees you again.

Done. Over it. Defeated.

You wish someone would take you by the hand and guide you through each step, making the big decisions easy. My friend, you aren't alone. **Are you ready to start planning your subscription box and finally create the business you've imagined? Yes!**

I know there can be a lot of questions and confusion when you're starting a subscription box business for the first time. If you don't have a plan to follow, it is easy to make critical mistakes, get off track, and quit before you send out those first boxes.

Without guidance and support, it can be difficult to make any progress at all! That's why I put together this book for you. Now you can start planning your subscription box and finally create the business you've imagined!

I'm here to tell you that you can do this! Just imagine what it will feel like when you've shipped your first boxes + finally get to deliver absolute delight to your new customers! Imagine the excitement of amazing reviews on your first box!

There is no doubt about it—the subscription box industry is hot! The market is healthy, is experiencing great growth, and like clockwork, the demand peaks around the holidays. So if you've got an idea that you think can make it, don't miss the chance to chase your dream! I grew my business, Sparkle Hustle Grow, a subscription box and online community for female entrepreneurs, into a full-time gig in under nine months with no prior product-based business experience. Even better, it is now a multi six-figure business that is changing the lives of small business owners every day.

I decided to create this book because the question I get more than any other is, "How do I start a successful subscription box?" In the following pages, I share the basic questions you need to work through to determine if a subscription box is the right path for you. By the time you reach the end, you will have clarity as to whether this idea is one you plan to pursue.

If you have a great idea for a box, that's fabulous! But it's just the beginning… you need a solid plan for how you're going to launch, grow, and scale your business. This book is your starting point and will guide you through the steps you'll need to carve out your subscription box business idea. However, before we get to that, it's really important that you first answer the question: WHY?

Ask yourself: Why do I want to start this box? That's the topic of the first chapter, because it's really important to know and understand.

I know it's cliche that everyone says *you have to start with your why*… but I want you to really understand how important this WHY is. Starting a subscription box changed the trajectory of my life. It was a lot of work, and, as I'll demonstrate in this book through my own stories and the stories of others, it's not always easy. Having a solid "why" will keep you motivated during tough times.

You could say that I'm a bit obsessed with subscription boxes and the financial freedom it brought my family. I believe everyone can gain the same freedom with the right guidance and support.

Thank you for choosing me to be your guide on this journey! I'm cheering you on! Share your pictures and progress on social media, tagging us *@subscriptionboxbootcamp*.

With gratitude,

Julie

How to Use this Book

This is your thirty day plan to get your subscription box idea off the ground. There are 15 chapters, many of which have workbook prompts. If you complete one chapter every other day (which is feasible, even with a busy schedule), you will be on track to have clarity by this time next month. You will have learned the basics of the subscription box industry, laid a solid foundation of your business idea, and will know your next steps.

Be sure to sign up for the companion guide at *subscriptionboxbootcamp.com/book-guide*.

There are pages at the end of each chapter for you to take notes and refer to as you progress through the exercises. If you come across any terms that you don't know, head over to Chapter Five where I break down some of industry terminology.

I believe there are five stages to your subscription box journey: Idea, Pre-Launch, Launch, Systems, and Scale. See the following image to learn more about each stage. In the big picture, this book represents the "Idea stage" of your subscription box journey.

Through exploration of the Idea stage, you will gain clarity around foundational concepts, including your niche, business name, product, and packaging, and also whether this subscription box business is something you wish to go forward with or not. No matter what stage you are in, you can find more resources at *subscriptionboxbootcamp.com*.

IDEA

Solidify your idea and build a foundation by learning the business model and carving out your concept. Do not move on until you understand how the sub box model works and you have identified your ICA, their pain point and how you will uniquely solve it.

PRE-LAUNCH

Establish your business operations while building the excitement around your upcoming launch. We recommend at least two months of pre-launch so you can build your audience on the front end, while you build out your business on the backend.

LAUNCH

You did it! You launched your subscription box business! This stage is both exciting and scary as you start to send your first boxes out into the world. This is a time of celebration, reflection and planning for the future.

SYSTEMS

Evaluate what's working + decide on your ongoing systems. This will allow you to lay the groundwork for a smooth monthly rhythm. Think of your business as a 30-day cycle and use that mindset to plan your weekly tasks.

SCALE

Now it's time to take your business to the next level by scaling your operations, reaching more people + getting out of your own way. Maybe that means outsourcing. Maybe that means creating an ad budget. Just remember, this isn't a race...get clear on your goals and put your plan in place to reach them!

"Happiness comes from what we do.
Fulfillment comes from why we do it."

— SIMON SINEK

CHAPTER 1
What's your Why?

A Little Bit of Backstory

You could say that the subscription box model has been a part of my life for decades, without me even realizing it. It all goes back to the story of Mid, the OG (Original Grandma) of subscription boxes. You're probably like, "What? Your grandma ran a subscription box?" Well, sort of. First let me paint the picture...

Mid was my Mom's mom. She was an amazing grandma to me and I have such fond memories of her. We called her Mawholla, which is the word "Maw" plus the shortened version of her last name, Varholla. So I'll reference her as Mawholla from here on out. She was strong in her faith and involved in her church, where she helped make amazing food like pierogi and nut rolls, some of my favorites. She was an entrepreneur in her own right. She'd make holiday cookies and then take them to the local health center and sell them to the employees. Then she'd use that money to buy gifts for patients or donate it to the activities fund.

Mawholla was married for over 50 years to my grandfather, George, but we called him Papholla. They lived right up the hill from us and I'd visit regularly, especially to go swimming with my brother and cousin, Seth. While we swam, the ladies played cards, oftentimes with the Steelers game in the background. The sounds of the game and the cards shuffling give me nostalgia to this day. Mawholla had a small frame, was tidy, stubborn (like me), tough, and always seemed well put together. She was a great family dinner host, especially on the holidays. When I eat those meals now, as an adult, it still makes me say, "This tastes like home."

Mawholla was a stay-at-home mom until her daughters (my mom and aunt) were older. She was in her thirties when she decided to get a job in retail at a clothing boutique. She learned to drive just to get to work and back; it was not the norm then for women to go to work. But she did it anyhow and it showed that she went after what she wanted despite the status quo, which I love.

She was quite trendy, so a gig at a local boutique made a natural fit. She was the best shopper around. The nearest good mall to us was a solid 45 minute drive away, and my Pap would drive us girls there and then sit and wait, taking our bags to the car every time we brought them back to him. He sat, content, on a bench in the mall chatting with the other guys. We would seriously shop till we dropped, using coupons and seeking out the best sales. She helped me pick outfits at stores like JCPenney, the Limited Too, Kaufmann's, and Kohl's. We both agreed that when we looked good, we felt good.

Every fall, we would get up at 4 a.m. for our annual Black Friday shopping trip, which was so much fun. It's evident that I got my retail therapy tendencies from that side of the family. I loved it and it created such great memories for us. Shopping was one big way that I bonded with Mawholla.

Hopefully by now, you have a picture painted in your head of this incredible woman. It makes me smile to tell this story. You probably want to know why she's the OG of subscription boxes. Well, you already know that she was my shopping buddy—my shopping mentor, if you will. So let's take it back to 1997 when I started college at Penn State. This was the first time I was away from my family for an extended period. Of course, there were lots of emotions. As a creative way for Mawholla and I to stay in touch, we'd send each other mail. Keep in mind, this was before email, text messaging, and video chats were the norm. For me, this mostly meant writing letters and sending cards to her. And I did this a lot. I knew that it made her feel really happy when she heard from me, so I kept cards and stamps handy.

Since shopping was kind of our thing, she'd send me fun surprises in the mail. Many times, it was a surprise piece of clothing. And funny, if you think about it, that's pretty much the whole StitchFix subscription model, to which I'm of course happily subscribed. Anyhow, she'd send me a shirt or a pair of pajamas or something fun like that.

But you know what article of clothing was the most fun? Underwear, or as we call them, gutchies (a western Pennsylvania thing). Yep, you heard that right. She'd send me cute gutchies in the mail. In the winter, I'd get gutchies with snowflakes or candy canes. For Halloween, it would be pumpkins. On Valentine's Day, they'd have hearts on them or maybe simple red lace. You get the point. Nothing racy, just cute. I'd get a new pair or two in the mail every month. It was so fun and she got the biggest kick out of it, like it was her goal to never send the same pair twice.

We had so much fun with it that she also started sending them to my roommates. Yup. She asked me everyone's sizes and was sure to have a fun new pair of gutchies for each one of them every month, even when I lived with five other amazing girl-friends. We were so excited when a box from Mawholla arrived! We'd gather at the table giggling as we opened the box. I know it sounds kind of silly, but we were broke college students and because Mawholla included the whole girl gang in on it, it was kind of like a bonding moment that we all got to share with her. It was so much fun!

So you see that by sending us new gutchies in the mail every month, my grandma earned the status of the OG, the Original Grandma, of subscription boxes. Nowadays there actually are underwear subscription boxes that are wildly successful! After all that time, can you believe that I send out monthly boxes for a living hoping to delight all of you each month like she delighted us?! It's so crazy to think about how things come back around. Who would've thought it?

Now that you know a little bit of the backstory of how the monthly mailer model has been a part of my life for decades, I thought we could move right into the story of how I launched Sparkle Hustle Grow in 2016…

My Subscription Box Launch Story

In 2011, I started my first business as a solopreneur. I worked in corporate America for more than a decade, climbing the ladder in sales and marketing jobs in the good old boys' club of the music industry and commercial radio. It was high stress—I remember how I'd get anxiety attacks on Sunday nights before starting the new week. The day that I got in trouble for wearing Converse Chucks to work, I knew I wasn't meant to be there. It wasn't for me anymore.

I was pregnant with my daughter, McKenna, and I was looking for a way out that would let me be myself, be there for my family, and still achieve my professional goals. I didn't want to work for somebody else anymore. I didn't want a long commute into the city. I was having a total mindset shift: I could build my own best workplace. In my second trimester I started freelancing on the side, doing internet marketing for small businesses. All I really needed to do this was an internet connection, a little bit of time to do the work, and eventually, a small group of women to support me. As I started to expand my client list, I reached out to other women who were also building their own freelance businesses in design, photography, and copywriting. We collaborated to support each other. I was building a solid digital marketing business called Grow Web Marketing. No need to Google it. I dissolved it shortly after going all in with Sparkle Hustle Grow.

By the summer of 2016, my web design firm was humming along, and since the work was location-independent, we decided to make a big change and move to a new city. The mountains were calling. Thanks to five years of hard work that I loved, we were able to move to the Asheville, North Carolina area the summer before McKenna started kindergarten. The natural beauty and amazing community was just what we dreamed of. But, as we were getting settled in our new home, I was beginning to feel unsettled in my work.

I was always behind the screen in digital work. I thrive in community, and, being in a new place, I was really missing that personal interaction. I was looking for my people - in the grocery store, at school, around town—even online. I wanted to find connection with others.

In my search to fill the emptiness I felt, I started dabbling in the idea of doing a product-based business—something tangible. So I thought... *How could I support other female entrepreneurs with a product?* What pain points could I solve? How could I be of value?

At the same time, it dawned on me that I love getting subscription boxes. I love getting *happy mail.*

That's really where the momentum really started—a subscription box with business tools and monthly trainings that would help female entrepreneurs thrive. This felt like a good business idea and one that really supported my greatest desire of being self-employed and still able to engage with others daily. I dreamed about a life of flexibility, allowing me to be present for my daughter when she was not in school, attend her activities, and to feel successful yet challenged. I also dreamed of earning enough money to retire my husband from his public school system job. I'm happy to report that I was able to do that too, sooner than expected. I was and still am 100% in on the entrepreneur life.

Later in this book, we'll be going into more details on how to determine what to include in your box and how to launch it, but first, I want to stress that it's not always easy, and your WHY needs to be strong to support you when the days are long and perhaps a bit challenging.

My WHY was strong. I wanted to build a life by design: one with flexibility, joy, personal and professional fulfillment, and connection with other women. I wanted to make an impact and have fun doing it. You may have a great idea for a box, but what is your WHY?

This first prompt is to help you refine your why, which may really help you refine your idea for your subscription box, as well as keep you going when the game gets tough.

STORIES
to inspire you

LAURA MORROW
Founder, Simply AIP
www.simplyaip.com

Three years ago, I started the Autoimmune Protocol (AIP) to help alleviate symptoms of what I now know is Lyme Disease. I was extremely fatigued and in pain, and totally revamping my diet and lifestyle was exhausting! I thought, "If only someone would just send me things that I can eat, where I don't have to figure out labels or make myself, life would be so much simpler!"

I started Googling around to find a meal delivery service or subscription box that could send me food, and to my surprise I couldn't find a single service or box that was AIP-compliant! So I decided that it was up to me to create what I had been searching for. I dove in head-first, absorbing everything I could about subscription boxes, business start-ups, online marketing, Facebook ads, and email lists. I discovered Sparkle Hustle Grow boxes pretty early, and I studied everything that Julie did to create a fantastic subscriber experience.

Two months after my initial idea, I created my first landing page and started running a Facebook ad. My goal was to collect 1000 emails before I opened my cart for business, but I wasn't sure exactly how that was going to happen. I was unknown in the AIP world and didn't even have an Instagram account yet, and to be honest I only knew a couple of people in real life that were following the AIP lifestyle. But I was determined to help other women take control of their health and manage their autoimmune symptoms.

The ads got a little bit of traction because a product for the AIP community was such a novel idea, but with gaining only a handful of new emails a day, I never felt like I was going to make it to my 1000 email goal. Then all of a sudden one night, I checked my Mailchimp account and started crying tears of joy—I had gained over 100 new emails in one day! Someone had shared one of my ads in an AIP Facebook group and the members had gone crazy over the idea! Momentum started to grow, and I reached 1000 email subscribers a couple of weeks later. I started my own Facebook group, and members were excited about the community and the upcoming box.

Things were going well, but I started to let fear creep in. My website still needed a lot of edits, and I realized that the April first launch date that I had been planning for months was Easter Sunday. Would anyone be paying attention to my website on that day? I started to think that maybe it was best if I delayed my launch by a week or two to make sure that I had everything perfect before going live.

Then four days before Easter Sunday, the unthinkable happened. The BIGGEST influencer in the AIP community sent out an email announcing that she had co-founded the first ever AIP subscription box and it was immediately open for orders! I literally couldn't believe it, and my world came crashing down. I had been working my butt off for four months, I had invested a few thousand dollars on my website and Facebook ads, and it felt like it had all been for nothing. I didn't believe that I could compete with someone who already had so much name recognition in the community. I had a total freak-out moment complete with sobbing and yelling, and I almost quit on the spot.

But then I thought about all the time and money that I had invested, and I figured that it would all be a total waste if I just quit, so I decided that I had no choice but to move forward. So I washed my face and put my makeup on while singing loudly along to Eminem's "Lose Yourself," and 10 minutes later I went Live on Facebook and announced that I was open for business on Sunday. The Live video was a hit with a lot of excitement, but I was still so scared of what would actually happen. I worked almost around the clock to get everything in place, including until 2:00 a.m. the night before trying to figure out glitches with the website.

I woke up that Sunday and went to church for Easter, nervous and excited all at the same time. At exactly noon I jumped on Facebook Live and counted down the last 10 seconds before I officially opened for business, and then hoped a couple of orders would trickle in... Ding! To my surprise, my email popped up with my first order just a minute later! Ding... ding... ding... and they kept coming in! My boys were running around the yard hunting Easter eggs with the neighborhood kids, and my email wouldn't stop dinging! Over 80 women subscribed to my box on that first day, and I sent out 124 boxes my first month in business. I'm so thankful that I didn't let a setback throw me totally off course, and I chose to keep going despite the obstacles.

A few months later, Julie started Subscription Box Bootcamp, and I was one of her first students. Even though I had a successful start, I knew that I had so much more to learn—and I wanted to learn from the best. Julie has been a fantastic mentor and has helped me navigate obstacles that have popped up along the way.

LEAH BRUSHETT
Founder & Head Hot Mess Mama
Mother Snacker

www.mothersnacker.com

I didn't have the easiest time transitioning into Motherhood. Like many moms experience but don't necessarily share, I suffered from postpartum anxiety, had a plate that was too full, was surviving off too little sleep, and didn't have any family nearby to help. After a long day of mommin' it, I loved settling down in the evening, indulging in the latest artisan sweet snack I had procured, and catching up on Netflix or Hulu. It was me-time that didn't require an appointment, weeks in advance to plan, or hiring a sitter. One evening it hit me, "Wouldn't it be cool if this type of experience was curated, packaged, and shipped right to a mom's door?"

I quickly got to researching and brainstorming. At the time there were a few mom-centric subscription boxes on the market but they all were either curated with baby products moms would love, like teethers, diaper rash cream, and lotions, or weighed heavily on lifestyle products from a "motherhood is beautiful" point of view—which yes, motherhood is beautiful, but let's be honest... sometimes it SUCKS and at the time there weren't any boxes coming from that point of view. Something a little more cheeky! So I did more research, some brainstorming, and web searches for trademarked names, and thus Mother Snacker was born.

I launched Mother Snacker about a year after the idea popped into my head. It took longer than expected but I spent my time learning and absorbing as much knowledge on the subscription box model as I could. I also was working full-time in the video game industry, was a mom to a precocious preschooler (I mean, aren't they all?), and had several personal life events that hindered a timely launch. But in the end, I think the timing for launch ended up just where it needed to be. I mention this part of the story because I want to be sure that if anyone is feeling discouraged from starting a business because they lack the time in their schedule or find that their plate feels too full, they can still build a business one small step at a time. You don't have to go at the speed anyone else is to find your own version of success.

SONDRA DIGGS
Girlfriend Relationship Advocate
Girlfriend Therapy in a Box
www.glittermethisco.com

As a divorced mom of two teenage girls, caretaker of aging parents, a CPA, and a corporate CFO of a multi-million dollar international company, life felt like I lived in a constant batting cage.

In just one year, I dealt with my mother having a stroke from Lupus, my father being diagnosed with Alzheimer's and aggressive prostate cancer, the loss of my longtime mentor and boss, and unexpected mental health issues with both of my teenage girls.

The only time I was truly happy was when I was hosting a party for my girlfriends.

The planning process alone was my prescription to control anxiety. I escaped into the details and the ultimate high came when I realized magic was happening. The dynamic of these women together was the greatest therapy anyone could ask for—hours of laughs, one-on-one chats, and secrets shared. Everyone bonded and left feeling a sense of relief and the feeling that their load was a little lighter.

I loved it so much that I wanted to box up that feeling and share it with the world. When I turned 50 I vowed to do what I am passionate about, so I hung up my calculator and took a leap of faith. That's the short version of my story but launching it was definitely a process. I had come across Sparkle Hustle Grow Box when I started thinking of creating a gift box. At the time, I had not narrowed into my true niche. I knew I loved hosting parties, I knew I loved doing it for my girlfriends and I knew I was bored with sending edible arrangements for every occasion. I was obsessed with glitter and when I Googled glitter box, Sparkle Hustle Grow came up. This box looked great because I had always been a corporate girl who now wanted to be a female entrepreneur, and of course as a CPA I knew exactly what she meant by "the best business expense ever." It immediately felt like the right place to start to get that motivation and knowledge. Ironically, the company I ran as a CFO was a subscription-based platform company for Loyalty Clubs, so I was super familiar with the revenue model.

After months of receiving her box, and still deeply thinking about how I could start a box full of glitter fun items, Julie announced she was starting a Bootcamp Course. I'll never forget that day, because I was already reaching out to people in my industry for connections, and spending hours on the internet trying to research how to do this very thing. It was like an answer from above saying, "Oh stop wasting time, girl, I have it all ready for you." I quickly signed up for her course and began the work. I had just spent a lot of money going to a trade show in New York a month before her course and was extremely discouraged because I ran around searching for anything with glitter, not realizing I wasn't truly in my purpose yet.

Her course started with helping you find your niche... this got me asking what my purpose was, what I wanted this box to do, and why would women want it. That is when the aha moment hit me. The core of me is a giver. I love giving gifts, and I loved giving to my girlfriends. The more I thought about my "why," the more I realized this wasn't supposed to be a monthly box of glitter items, but a gift box filled with items specific to the needs of your girlfriend because you couldn't be there to show up for her in-person. I knew I wanted to make her smile. At that moment, while sitting in my CFO office, I grabbed a piece of paper, wrote S.M.I.L.E., filling in the word with how it feels to be out with your girlfriends. This is how Sparkle, Move, Indulge, Laugh, and Exhale was birthed. Yes, I know I went a different direction from the subscription model out the gate, but Julie's course directed every move I still had to make, and continues to do so today. She truly needs to know how her purpose to help other women has succeeded!

WORKBOOK

Prompt

WHAT'S YOUR WHY?

Journal your thoughts on the biggest motivating factors behind becoming a subscription box entrepreneur. Write freely, but go into detail about what you want to change in your life now and how you envision your best life. Write about how you feel now and how you want to feel in the future, keeping your why in focus. It may look messy at first, but I want you to have clarity and resolve around *your why,* so that you can come back to it when times are tough.

_____

_____

_____

_____

_____

_____

_____

_____

_____

_____

_____

_____

_____

WHAT'S YOUR WHY?

"There's so much love
sent through the mail."

— SHERIDAN HAY

CHAPTER 2

What's so great about subscription boxes?

Can you imagine being the BEST part of someone's day... month after month? How something you dreamed up and put together could make a powerful, positive difference in someone's life? Yes please! I want you to think of your subscription box business opportunity as something much bigger than just a box. I've had people tell me stories about how one item in my box led to an amazing conversation, which led to someone hiring them, and that led to putting food on the table for their family. Talk about impact. AND the more money you make, the more impact you can have on those around you. I'm very motivated by the prospect of helping others, generously donating to great causes, and treating my team to beach retreats—"work hard, play hard" is one of our driving principles! And a subscription box made this all possible.

All dreams have to be grounded with some hard work and dedication though, right? So let's get started on that. This chapter is dedicated to helping you learn the basics of the subscription box industry and what drives it.

What exactly IS a subscription box?

In its simplest form, it's a recurring shipment—usually in a box, as you might have guessed—that includes products based around a common theme, category, interest, or need. There's a box for every category you can think of. There's coffee boxes, crafting crates, boxes of makeup, men's grooming boxes, self-care crates, and so much more.

What you'll find is that most subscription boxes are delivered monthly, but some are delivered seasonally or quarterly. This means that the customer is charged on a regular schedule to continue receiving the product. That's the biggest difference between a subscription box product versus a regular e-commerce product. It's on a recurring model.

So what's in it for the business owner?

Some benefits of this recurring revenue model include:

- Consistent, predictable income. Once you get started, it's easy to use your analytics to make fairly accurate projections.

- Increased return on customer acquisition costs. You spend money to acquire every customer you have. Wouldn't it be nice to know they are going to stick around month after month, rather than having to find another new customer to sell the same product to?

- You can earn more through upselling and cross-selling. Your subscribers already know and love you, so it's easy to introduce new or complimentary products to them, as they are already primed to buy.

- Manageable stock control. You set the limits on how many boxes you will make available each month. Don't sell them all? Not to worry! There are plenty of ways to offload excess inventory.

- It's an automated business, meaning you can set up your systems and it will work like clockwork each month. Don't get me wrong, this is not a passive income stream. There are a lot of moving parts to a subscription box business, but the predictable and recurring nature of the model helps make it manageable.

WHY PEOPLE LOVE SUBSCRIPTION BOXES

What's not to love? There are so many reasons! The experience of a subscription box is so much fun! Here are some of the common reasons subscribers give as to why they love being a member.

The element of surprise

When you get a box of surprise items, it's like opening a gift at the holidays, or opening a birthday present. It's just plain fun! The element of surprise can really delight a customer as they are unboxing all the new goodies. And everyone likes getting mail that isn't a stack of bills, am I right? As a box owner, our goal is to make sure that it's a curated experience and that the items bring value and joy to your subscriber, keeping them hooked so they stick around month after month.

Product discovery

No matter what your passion is, you're always looking to discover something new about it. Consumers use subscription boxes as a way to discover new products! It can be a great way to learn about new product lines or new brands that you might not have found in your local stores or online. For example, if you really love makeup or if you blog about beauty, subscribing to a makeup box will expose you to new products and ideas that you may not otherwise get access to. Sometimes box companies are able to get exclusive products made just for them, adding a whole new layer of discovery and exclusivity.

The experience

A person might subscribe to a box because of experiential factors beyond what product is in there. Experiential factors may include, for example, access to a community of like-minded people, exclusive discounts, or bonuses such as digital downloads or playlists. There are a variety of things that you can add above and beyond the products to make your box more valuable and truly an experience.

Convenience

Once upon a time before the internet, we had to go to different stores or shop from catalogs and order over the phone. Now we can get any product quickly delivered to our door at a competitive price. Since people have no problem getting exactly what they want exactly when they need it, retailers can take it to the next level and give them what they want without even asking. These are a special kind of subscription box called a "replenishment-style box." A member of one of these subscription boxes automatically receives replenishments of the products they love. My box bestie Jessica runs the All Girl Shave Club, which sends razors, refills, and shave butter just as you need them. It's automatic, convenient, and feels like such a luxury!

Trust

People want an expert, someone they can trust to provide them with the RIGHT items month after month. This really depends on your niche. For example, they trust me and my team to deliver the best personal development and business training. If you have a box for pets, like Kait and Jess from the Bunny Fun Box, you would provide the best snacks, toys, and accessories for bunny owners. Talk about niching down, right? People crave connection with like-minded people and one way they fulfill that craving is through subscribing to boxes that fulfill this need. If they buy your product, they trust you to deliver the best of the best in your box's particular category.

The consumer experience is such an important part of your success as a subscription box owner, and needs to be at the forefront of your planning. As a subscription box coach, I conduct a lot of market research. This means I subscribe to many boxes—not only because I love getting them, but also because I want to remind myself of the consumer experience when I get a new box. I want to remember that feeling of delight when the box is amazing, and I want to remember that feeling of disappointment when the box falls short. These experiences are super helpful as a business owner and I try to tap into those feelings when I'm curating Sparkle Hustle Grow.

Of all the boxes I've received, none have impressed me more than those from my Subscription Box Bootcamp students. The ideas they are launching into the world are changing lives. Like Black Girl MATHgic, designed to increase math confidence and decrease math anxiety in girls on a third to eighth grade math level, and Mother Snacker, which makes motherhood sweeter one box at a time by delivering decadent sweet treats and encouraging notes to moms. It's exciting that these students are proving we can do something we love with our subscription boxes and make a difference in the lives of our subscribers.

Now that we've covered why both business owners and customers love subscription boxes, take a minute to reflect on your own experience with subscription boxes. I love this workbook prompt because it's important to remember the delight of a great box experience and the disappointment of a bad box experience. You can reflect on those feelings as you begin to build your own subscription box concept.

WORKBOOK

Prompts

1. What are some of your favorite subscription boxes and why?

2. How do you feel when you open those boxes? Write down the good and the bad. You will want to keep these answers in mind every time you are selecting products for your own subscription box.

_____

_____

_____

_____

_____

_____

_____

_____

_____

_____

_____

_____

_____

_____

WHAT'S SO GREAT ABOUT SUBSCRIPTION BOXES?

"Today is a good day
to learn something new."

— AUTHOR UNKNOWN

CHAPTER 3
How does the subscription box model work?

The subscription box model has a lot of moving parts, including sourcing, customer service, marketing, and retention. Understanding the model can be a bit overwhelming but trust me, it's worth it. Knowing the basics before you invest in your new business will help you build a solid foundation and set you up for faster success. Before you actually start a subscription box, you need to understand how the box model works, since it's different from other business models. In this chapter, we are going to cover the two main categories of boxes and the two main shipping options.

Subscription boxes fall into two main categories: **product discovery** and **replenishment**.

Product discovery boxes help subscribers experience exciting new products, as you might imagine. Think of this model as the surprise pack or grab bag, based around the box's theme or category. My subscription box, Sparkle Hustle Grow, is a perfect example of this. I supply female entrepreneurs with incredible business tools and supplies, from colorful paper clips and fancy pens to detailed trainings, all designed to help them grow their businesses. I laugh in delight as subscribers discover new products they never heard of that now they can't live without! It's very fulfilling when your subscribers go wild over the products you curated for them!

Some boxes include products that are important to someone with lifestyle needs who may not have the time to find all the latest products, snacks, or tools—like my friend Laura's Simply AIP box, which is a special delivery for people following the Autoimmune Protocol diet. Those subscribers are overjoyed each month to find new snacks, products, and ideas to supplement their diet and lifestyle.

Replenishment-style boxes make sure we never run out of the things we need each month. We don't want to be left hanging when we've run out of toothpaste or need a fresh razor. For this type of box, your goal is to meet an anticipated need, which is really appealing in a go-go-go world where we really like the idea of taking things off our plates. Think about the Amazon Subscribe and Save model, where you can sign up for the products you need to be delivered to you in the schedule that makes sense; for example, a giant bag of dog food once a month, or coffee every two weeks. Resupplying the items we consume on a regular basis through an automatic shipment reduces the need to think about whether or not we'll have enough dish detergent or eye makeup.

DETERMINING SHIPPING SCHEDULE

Once you've decided whether your box will be primarily discovery (sharing new products for them to try) or replenishment (resupplying a specific need each month), you'll need to determine the shipping schedule.

There are two main types of shipping schedules, or what we call "fulfillment" batch shipping or ongoing shipping. It's important to decide early which of the two shipping schedules you wish to use because it impacts both your business plans and setting appropriate customer expectations. Many logistical and marketing decisions will be made on the basis of which shipping schedule you choose.

Batch shipping is when you choose a specific day in your operational life cycle (the day-to-day tasks) and ship all subscription orders at once on that day. Every customer from that point forward will renew on the same date each month.

Pros of batch shipping

One of the best things is that you pick, pack, and ship in a batch, which is super efficient. Just set up your workspace like an assembly line for maximum efficiency. If all boxes contain the same products, they can be packed quickly. The more variations you have, the more complicated it gets, but in general, batch shipping is efficient.

Predictable revenue cycles make cash flow and projections easier. When renewal day hits on that same day, every single month, you know when you're going to have your bank account replenished with that cash flow.

You will have the ability to plan customer service needs in line with your cycle. At Sparkle Hustle Grow, we know that we will have increased customer service needs on a few very specific days of the month. For example, the day before and after our renewal day and shipping day tend to be heavy customer service days.

Cons for batch shipping

You may feel that it's a lot of work to pack all the shipments at one time, especially if you are a solopreneur. So, while batch shipping is efficient, it can be overwhelming when it's time to prep all your boxes for shipment at once.

Some customers have to wait a really long time for their first package, depending on when they order. For example, if they ordered on the first day of the sales cycle, they are going to wait about a month to get their box if you only ship once a month. This can lead to frustrated customers, a higher churn (turnover) rate, and higher customer service needs with people contacting you asking where their box is. However there are ways to combat this by setting expectations. Use email marketing, Facebook group interaction (if you have a group), and of course, making sure that the product is worth waiting for and your customer is delighted when they receive it. Some box owners combat this long wait with a welcome box. If you do this, be aware that you have to make room in the budget for this extra box.

Ongoing shipping, also known as anniversary shipping, means that you will ship as new orders come in and each customer will then renew on the anniversary of their specific signup date. Example: the customer orders a box on November first. It's processed and shipped to arrive within a few days of the order. The account will renew 30 days later on December first, for a monthly subscription.

Pros of ongoing shipping

Customers get their packages faster. That's a huge win. That can result in a better customer experience since nobody likes to wait. Thanks to Amazon Prime shipping, we all expect to receive items lighting fast.

Quick shipping generally results in a better customer experience, leading to increased likelihood of more return purchases and fewer cancellations. A lower cancellation rate is money in the bank, and it's definitely cheaper to keep a customer than to get a new one.

You have a constant stream of revenue with an ongoing shipping model. You won't have to wait for your cash injection on renewal day since you'll get renewals coming in every single day.

Cons of ongoing shipping

You have to pick, pack and ship those boxes constantly. There are ways to manage it though, and you can find balance by designating shipping days once or several times a week.

Inventory management can be complex. With ongoing shipping, you now have a constant flow of products coming in and going out the door. At some point you have to decide when you're moving onto the next month's products or the next month's box assortment, while at the same time you may have excess inventory. It can be a hard balance to figure out.

Now that we've covered both pros and cons, which way are you leaning? Batch shipping or ongoing shipping? One of these options might be an obvious choice for you but, if not, think about what will provide the best customer experience. If you still aren't sure, think about if anything is time sensitive. For example, Sparkle Hustle Grow is a guided box experience, where we walk our customers through a series of events, so it's time sensitive. Those boxes need to get in my customer's hands at the same time because we do a monthly book study and online business training. As a group, our subscribers work through these books and training with the guidance of guest experts and moderators in the private Facebook group. Because of this, it's important for all of my subscribers to receive their box around the same time so that we can dive in together. But if you don't need your customers to receive their boxes at the same time, then ongoing shipping might be a good option for you.

The next decision you need to make is how often you want to ship your subscription box to your customers. Are you going to ship monthly, quarterly, or seasonally? **Cratejoy, one of the leaders in the subscription box industry, reports that the most successful boxes are monthly boxes.** There is more top-of-mind awareness, more frequent renewal dates (which means cash injections in your business), and it's easier to plan for inventory. But that doesn't mean you have to offer a monthly box. For a custom schedule, you may need to tweak a few things in your ecommerce software to work with your specific calendar. Again, I urge you to think about which option would best suit your customers based on the nature of the contents of the box.

Now that you've had a chance to think about the type of box and when it will ship, it's time for you to make some decisions and put it on paper. Fill out the following workbook prompts before moving onto the next chapter.

WORKBOOK

Prompts

1. What type of box do you want to create (product discovery or replenishment) and why?

2. How often do you want to ship your boxes and why?

3. Will you batch ship or ship on an ongoing basis?

"I could have started my subscription box years ago if I could have conquered my fear and doubt. I have now taken that leap of faith, so here I go!"

— MELODEE ABEE, FOUNDER OF KINDTUDE

CHAPTER 4
Getting Started

Just start. That sounds way too easy, doesn't it?

You have permission to do this thing! So often we have big goals and big dreams, but we're paralyzed with fear: fear of being judged, fear of failing, fear of the technology required. I've been there!

OK, so I recognize it's more than me saying: Just Start!

Because you need more direction with the HOW part, right?

So let's start with the tools and information you need to **start and run** a subscription box business. In this chapter, I hope to provide the basics, save you a ton of time scouring the internet to figure out exactly what you need to get started, and reduce your overwhelm around launching a subscription box business.

Before we get into the specifics of the box itself, a little heads up. You will be ahead of the game if you already have some kind of experience in the business space. If you don't, it's not a deal breaker, it may just take you a little longer to move through some of these pieces. Think about it this way; if you have an existing audience, you can announce your box and start building the hype for launch. But if you are starting from scratch, it will take a little extra time to build your audience so you have someone to launch to. Like most businesses, this is not a "build it and they will come" scenario.

I was so worried about what people would think of my business;
that they would think it's dumb or unnecessary. I wish I hadn't been so
afraid of failure because it nearly paralyzed me. And I wish I had been
OK with rejection in the early days; instead, it really affected me!

—JENN COLLINS, CHIEF SELF-CARE OFFICER
Mama Needs Box + Podcast Host
www.mamaneedsbox.com

Here are the things you need, at a minimum, to begin your subscription box business.

1. A computer, a printer, and internet access. This is a no-brainer for a web-based business, but we're going through the full checklist. What I need you to understand is that it's more than having access to a computer. You're going to need a *reliable* computer, printer, and internet connection. You're going to be selling your product, your subscription box, online. You need to be able to get online regularly, check your sales, make changes in the backend of the software and make sure that your business is running smoothly.

You need a printer, too, because if you're selling something you're going to ship, then you need to be able to print labels. I recommend a thermal printer, which uses heat activation to print so it doesn't need any ink in it. I'll provide links in your book companion guide found at *subscriptionboxbootcamp.com/book-guide*. When I first started, I used a basic black and white printer, with print-at-home self-stick package labels. You don't need a fancy, expensive printer and high-end computer from day one, you just need to make sure that you have a reliable computer, internet access, and a way to print out those labels.

2. A unique box concept that solves a pain point in a specific niche. What pain point does your box help someone overcome? Providing a solution to something makes you valuable in your ideal customers' eyes, making it a no-brainer to subscribe. If you don't know how to figure this out, you will learn all of this information in later chapters, so don't panic. I am going to show you exactly how to get clarity on this very important topic.

3. Cart software. You must have a cart! You can't just launch a website and take orders. There's a whole process that's going on behind the scenes called cart software and, when we're selling subscription boxes, it needs to be a *recurring* cart software. It's specifically made for products that renew on a certain schedule. To do that, it automatically charges your subscribers on a recurring basis for each month's new order.

When a new customer signs up, they get charged immediately for their order. Then when they hit their renewal date, the recurring cart software will post their next order and credit card charge automatically. Not all ecommerce software is set up to do this. At Sparkle Hustle Grow, we use Cratejoy, which is both a marketplace for subscription box businesses and an all-in-one software for the subscription box business owners. You can take orders, build your website, buy postage, and even run emails through the Cratejoy software. Whatever solution you choose, software is one of those startup costs that you will have to cover.

4. Email marketing software. This software helps you gather email addresses and build your lists so that you have people to communicate with and market to, all of which will help you promote your box. Ideally, your email marketing software will allow you to segment your list, so you can send different email messages to different types of people on your list. For example, you may want to send a weekly update to subscribers, and then send a marketing email to a different segment (i.e. leads) to offer them a first-box discount. We love Flodesk, but have used Mailchimp and Convertkit in the past. You will want to choose an email marketing service provider that is compatible with your cart software. We use Cratejoy + Flodesk at Sparkle Hustle Grow.

5. Boxes, tape and packing materials. No big surprise, right? After all, you are selling a subscription *box*. We use Givr-Pack to print our custom printed boxes, which is also popular with many of our Subscription Box Bootcampers. GivrPack has great customer service, plus they plant 20 times more trees than they use to make our boxes. I love that commitment to sustainability. While my company uses custom boxes, you don't have to do that at launch if you choose not to. There are so many other options. For example, you could buy plain boxes. They come in different colors and you can buy them at places like Staples, Uline, or Amazon. Then you can take that plain box and add your branding.

A great, easy option is to use custom stickers. We love Sticker Mule for custom stickers. Just slap that sticker on top—instant custom branding! We also use Sticker Mule for custom poly mailers for some of our smaller packages and packing tape branded with our logo, which looks really professional. They're a great partner because they have quality items that ship really fast. If you really don't have much of a budget, you can start very easily with plain boxes paired up with branded stickers.

No matter how you design your box exterior, you'll also need tape and packing materials. Mailer-style boxes typically have a flap that you close, but you still need to secure it so it doesn't open up in transit. You can use basic shipping tape, branded stickers, or wafer seals.

For packing materials, there are plenty of choices. We use crinkle cut paper in our boxes. I love that it holds things in place so the box isn't all jumbled up with products everywhere. It also protects the products with a little bit of padding in case it gets bumped around during shipping, which is especially important if you have fragile items. We use pretty, eye-catching metallic crinkle cut, and it enhances the user experience. When they open up that box and they see this beautiful shiny packaging and all the products neatly placed in there, it contributes positively to our brand and is part of the SHG unboxing experience. There are so many ways you can establish branding through packaging. You could use tissue paper to wrap the products, then put a sticker on top to keep the tissue shut. It's a really inexpensive choice for your packing material. Or you could use bubble wrap or air pillows, especially if you are shipping something fragile like candles or mugs.

6. Products. The products that you're going to pick are the hero of the box. They're the reason people keep coming back. You'll want to have a unique mix of products to keep customers excited and eager to unbox it every single month. Make sure there's different sizes and weights of products, and that the products are cohesive. For example, you could choose a color scheme, a monthly theme, or products that are complementary to each other. We want to make sure that they look good together because this can have a strong influence on the positive impact of the perceived value during the unboxing experience.

By far one of most frequent questions I am asked is, "Where do you get your products? How do you approach vendors and get the best prices?" In Chapter 10, we'll go into a lot of details about sourcing your products. It's important to know that you don't really have to buy everything before you launch. In Chapter 13, we'll talk about holding a pre-sale, which is something I found super helpful. A private pre-sale helped me earn some startup funds, which was crucial since I basically had a zero dollar budget for launching my box. More on that later!

7. Time to commit. This is not a get-rich-quick scheme. It won't happen overnight. This is something that you need to commit to. You want to treat your subscription box business like a business, not a hobby. That being said, it absolutely can be a side hustle. I know so many people who run their box business as a side hustle while they're working full time or staying at home with the kids. As you may remember from my own story, that's actually how I started Sparkle Hustle Grow. It was a side hustle and then within nine months I was able to turn it into my full-time gig, which was so exciting. But you don't have to make it full-time if that's not your goal. This is your race. You are not running against anyone but yourself. If your goal is to have a side hustle and earn a part-time income, that's totally doable, but it's important to remember that it still takes time to commit. That's partly why I've seen so much success with our students at Subscription Box Bootcamp. I've laid out the roadmap for them to be successful and make better use of their time. They don't waste time scouring the internet anymore, piecing together training videos, blogs, and random information, and getting stuck in decision fatigue. I hope this book will help you in the same way. You don't need to be full-time, but you need time, energy, and drive to commit to your own success.

Sometimes all we need to do is make that first step
in making our dreams a reality.

—SHONDA RAMSEY, FOUNDER
Say It With Grace
www.sayitwithgracebox.com

WORKBOOK

Prompts

Let's check in before we move on.

1. Do I have what I need to start? If not, think of ways you can access what you need (purchase, borrow, find an investor to help with startups). Where there's a will, there's a way!

   - Write down what you already have.
   - Write down what you still need. Brainstorm how you will solve fulfilling those needs.

2. Will you make the time to commit to going through this book and moving forward into launching your subscription box business? Let *your why* motivate you. Do like Dolly Parton and pour yourself a cup of ambition! In your calendar or planner, block out a few hours a week to do the work in this workbook and take the necessary action steps.

_____

_____

_____

_____

_____

_____

"Industry jargon may not be a language your customer understands."

— RON KAUFMAN

CHAPTER 5

The Lingo

Like any other industry, subscription boxes have their own terminology, with meanings that might be a little different from other uses. The goal of this chapter is to make sure you're aware of common terminology and what they'll mean to YOU in this business. You might have to read through this chapter once and refer back to it when you are approaching your launch date. This is not an all-inclusive list, but rather a hand-picked list of terms that might not be as common or familiar.

Pre-launch is the early phase of launching your box before you have anything actually to sell. It's the way to generate buzz and excitement around your business, and also a great source of early feedback.

Why is pre-launch important?

Building your foundation: Pre-launch is a time where you are building the foundation of your business, such as branding, researching vendors, building your website, and niching down your idea.

Validation: This is so important! So often we think we know what our customers want, but we really need to *ask* them. You'd be surprised what information that they're willing to give you, so here's your chance to listen to them. You'll be able to validate your business idea or figure out where you need to tweak it before you launch.

Building an audience: When you're launching your business, you can't just launch to an empty room and expect to earn revenue and be successful. By building an audience in advance, you actually have someone to market to. Tell them when you're launching, tell them where you are in the process, and keep communicating. It is critically important to get to know them and ask them questions to determine how you can meet their needs. If you don't build your audience at the beginning, then you can't expect to have a successful launch.

Prototype your box: Mock up a sample box. You can use this to play around with product assortment and even use it in marketing. The products you put in your prototype don't have to be what you offer in your launch. Rather, include *the type* of products and brands you want, so your audience will get an idea of what to expect. It can be as simple as picking up a few items in local stores. Don't overthink it.

Operational life cycle Terms

We will cover this more in-depth in another chapter, but it's important so I'm sharing it here too. You need to understand the life cycle of your subscription box so that you can create systems around it, as well as communicate it with your customers.

The **Open Cart date** or first date of your sales cycle is when a new box is available. Oftentimes business owners use each month as a sales cycle (1st-->31st), to keep it simple and intuitive for the customer. If you are batch shipping, think of your sales cycle as the time when customers are reserving their next box. So for example, you would be (pre)selling the April box from March 1st through March 31st.

Whatever sales cycle dates you decide on, the last day of your sales cycle for any given box is your **Cut-off date**. That means it's the last day for your customers to subscribe to that box. So for example, if your cut-off date is March 31st for the April box, a customer that subscribed on April 1st would be reserving their May box since they just missed the cut-off date for the April box. If you ship daily/weekly (instead of in batches), your dates might look a little different, but you still need to decide on the dates you want to switch to your next box assortment.

You'll also need to set your **Renewal date**, or your rebilling date, since your product has a recurring billing date. If you are batch shipping, you will renew all active subscribers on this date. If you are anniversary shipping (or ongoing shipping), each customer will have a renewal date based on their initial purchase.

The **Shipping date** is when you fulfill your customer's orders. If you batch ship, this will likely fall on one specific day each month, for example, the 4th of the month. If you do ongoing shipping, the shipping date is not as pertinent to your operational life cycle.

Tracking Performance

There are three main **KPIs—key performance indicators**, or important data specific to the subscription box industry that helps you gauge your success. You'll want to check these regularly. You'll start to notice trends month after month.

Churn: Churn is the percent of subscribers that cancel each month. I look at our churn rate almost every day. The lower the churn rate, the better. For a frame of reference, at Sparkle Hustle Grow, I typically shoot for 10% or less. This means if you have one hundred subscribers and you have a 10% churn rate, on average you will lose 10 subscribers per month.

Retention: The opposite of churn is retention, or the percent of customers that renew each sales cycle. In other words, it's customers that you keep. In the same example of 10% churn, that means you would retain 90% of your subscribers each month—90 of those 100 subscribers in our example.

Average duration: This is the average number of days your subscriber stays active. The longer the better. From the average duration, you can figure out the lifetime value of a customer. Average duration also helps to determine how much you're willing to spend on advertising to acquire that customer. If the average customer spends three months as a subscriber and your subscription box costs $50, you know that their lifetime value is $150. Knowing and understanding average duration will help you continue to grow and will help strategize marketing, customer retention and goal setting.

Operations Terms

As I mentioned previously, there are a lot of moving parts in a subscription box business. I'll walk you through more operations elements in later chapters, but there are a few important operational terms I want to cover here, in case they might be new to you.

A **Fulfillment Center** is a third party vendor that you can hire to handle your order fulfillment. They will accept deliveries on your behalf and they will provide a team to build, pack, and ship your boxes. You can also call this a warehouse or a 3PL, which stands for third party logistics. You will probably start by fulfilling in-house, but may want to consider using a fulfillment center around the 250 subscriber mark.

Variations are different product assortments that you can include in your subscription box. For example, you might send different sized items (i.e. small, medium, large). Or maybe you offer multiple colors of the same item. These are all variations. As you can imagine, things become more complex when you include variations. I encourage you to proceed with caution and keep it as simple as possible. The more complex or customized you make it, the more difficult fulfillment will be for you, and the more costly it will be for a fulfillment center to process. There is also more room for error.

Payment processor. You want to get paid, right? Then you have to have a payment processor to handle the transactions. When someone uses a debit card or a credit card, they are going through a third party. We use and recommend Stripe. It collects the payment for you and then transfers it to your bank account, usually after a few days. Most payment processors have a transaction fee, instead of a monthly fee. This means you only pay the fee when you make a sale. This is all automatic when you integrate your payment processor and your online shop.

One of the things that I always tell aspiring subscription box owners is to keep it simple to start. I know you have a million amazing ideas, and that's awesome! But, it's so much better to start with one product or one niche, instead of launching with a lot of complexities right away.
I started out with 4 different subscription offers and it was a LOT of work! We eventually simplified it, by listening to the feedback of our subscribers and cutting the options that weren't as popular or profitable.
It would have saved me a lot of time and stress if I had just launched with one initial offer, and let my customers' feedback shape it along the way.

—JESSICA PRINCIPE, FOUNDER
All Girl Shave Club
www.AllGirlShaveClub.com

"Defining your target market or niche
is the single most important business decision
you can make as an entrepreneur."

— SASKIA GREGORY

CHAPTER 6
Carve out your Concept

Success in this business will come from spending the time to research and understand your niche. It's one thing to have a light bulb moment for your box idea, but, before you launch, you will need to clarify your box idea, identify who you'll serve, and figure out how you'll solve their pain points.

Carving out your concept is one of my favorite things to do with the students in my Subscription Box Bootcamp. If you're like most new box dreamers, you probably have all these great ideas that you're thinking about, but you're going to need some clarity to move forward.

At the end of this chapter, you'll find a workbook prompt to help you write down all the things you need to dig deeper into. And bonus: this work is the beginning of your business plan.

In this chapter, I'll explain all the pieces you need to know and understand to complete the prompts. As you go through these exercises, keep your notes handy at the end of this chapter.

Your Niche

Who do you want to reach with your box? What is the overall niche of your box? A "niche" refers to the products, services, or interests that appeal to a small, very specialized section of the population. We're not going to use broad terms like women or men as an audience—we're going to go a little bit deeper.

As an example, let's look at Sparkle Hustle Grow. Sure, it's for women, but it's specifically for ambitious women business owners in the United States. One step further: it's more specifically for a newer female entrepreneur who is looking for tools and resources to help grow her business. That's a much more specific niche than just "female business owners."

To serve a niche best, you need to really clearly define it. Instead of choosing a niche for moms, maybe it's working moms with young kids. You get the point. A great example of this is the Peaceful Play box by Subscription Box Bootcamper Stephanie. This box is for work- and stay-at-home moms of preschoolers to seven-year-olds and empowers them to use independent play instead of screens to keep their kids busy! Brilliant!

When you think you've got the niche identified, niche down, niche down, and niche down one more time. Meaning, get even MORE specific on who they are. Once you've identified that very specific audience, you can create an ICA, or ideal client avatar, or persona. It refers to the one very specific person that is your ideal target buyer. You want to identify as many details as possible about this person. It may seem weird at first, but it's helpful to establish this clarity. When you create your product and when you strategize your marketing efforts, you can imagine that you are talking directly to this one person you've detailed so fully.

There's a common misconception in marketing that the larger the audience you can sell to the better, but I really believe that subscription box businesses and most other businesses in general, should narrow it down to their exact target audience. That way, it's an easier sell. Instead of trying to sell to the hundreds of thousands of people that might have this one similar interest, you will be marketing to a smaller audience, but it will be an easier sell because when they come across your box for the first time, they're going to know that that box was made just for them. Of course there will be outliers, meaning you will have buyers that don't fit the specs of your target audience, but that's okay! The more focus you have on your specific niche, the easier it will be to solve their problems, delight them with your products, and ultimately make that next sale.

As a buyer, when you see a product that feels like it was made for you, it makes it so much easier to pull out your credit card and buy it with no remorse. You're aiming for this level of clarity with the person you're marketing to. What would make the box feel like it was made just for them?

YOUR BOX NAME

If you're like me, you probably have an entire notebook full of business name ideas. If not, now is the time to brainstorm all your box name ideas. By the end of this chapter, I want you to have landed on your box name. So exciting!

Get creative and think about a name that will really explain what your box is, but also resonate with your audience. Many people will include the word box or crate in their business name, but it's certainly not required. Take Subscription Box Bootcamper Laura for example. She created a box focused on food, fun, and female empowerment and named it Laura's Kitchen Table! How creative!

Consider whether the name has been used before. If there are some business names that are very similar to what you have as your business name at this point, I would highly recommend that you reconsider and try to come up with a name that's a little more unique. Trust me, you don't want to have to change your box name after you've already launched.

- Check Google
- Check social media platforms
- Check the USPTO (United States Patent and Trademark Office)

Here's a few tips on choosing a name:

- You want it to be unique.
- You want it to speak directly to the audience that you're serving so that when they read it, they know what it is and know it was made just for them.
- Make it easy to spell and read.
- Ask your target audience for feedback.
- Google search your business name idea with a hashtag in front of it to make sure it's not already associated with something that doesn't align with you, especially if you are using abbreviations or slang in your business name. That could be risky territory.

Back in the spring 2019 I was really evaluating what I wanted to do professionally. As a stay at home mom and working in direct sales, I knew I wanted something different and wanted it to be centered around food and female small businesses. I toyed with the idea of blogging, but that didn't excite me. In the fall of 2019, I came across a post that had Julie Ball and her subscription box business. The lightbulb basically exploded! I had to do a subscription box with food/beverage items exclusively from female-owned small businesses.

—LAURA KOCKLER, FOUNDER AND CEO
Laura's Kitchen Table
www.lauraskitchentable.com

Once you've done your brainstorming and research, land on that business name and write it down at the end of this chapter.

YOUR WEBSITE ADDRESS

Next, we're going to talk about your website address, also known as your URL or domain name. It's where you will send people when you want them to subscribe. To check if a domain is available, I recommend two places. First, simply type it in your web browser to see if it's live and in use from someone else. Second, if it isn't, then head over to namecheap.com and search there. If it's available, great—grab it! Most domains I've searched for were under $20 a year to own, so it's not expensive.

The exact name of your box might not be available but don't panic. It's possible that someone has it and they want to sell it for a very high price. Think this decision through before you do this because your URL doesn't just have to be your box name. For example, there's a kid's cooking box called Raddish and their URL is raddishkids.com. It's actually really smart because people immediately know that it's a box for kids. You could add the word boxes after your business name, like thinkoutsideboxes.com does, or maybe you add monthly after the box name. You could also add the word "my" in front of the box name to make it feel a little personal, like Subscription Box Bootcamp student LaTonya, founder of myrenewbox.com.

Here are my tips for choosing a domain name:

- Keep it short: really easy way to do that would be maybe just using the name of your box dot com. If that's not available, then you can get creative. So it could be yourboxmonthly.com.It could be getyourbox.com.
  It could be a call to action or some sort of a phrase that your target audience would resonate with. It could also be your tagline.

- Consider using keywords in your domain name. That way it'll be better for search engine optimization (SEO). In other words, it is easier for Google to pick you up and put you in the listings.
- When you're making your domain name choice, you want to try and get a dot com because that's the most popular and the most memorable extension.
- If you have the budget for it, go ahead and buy the dot net, the dot org, the dot whatever you want, so you can secure that name and someone else doesn't get it, however, it's not required by any means.
- You want to make sure that your domain name is easy to type and spell. In other words, don't choose a word that is commonly misspelled. Make it easy for someone to actually find your website.
- Avoid numbers and hyphens.

STORIES
to inspire you

BRITTANY RHODES
Founder & General MATHager
Black Girl MATHgic
www.blackgirlmathgic.com

It all started in 2014, when I met a young man who is now my husband. When we first began dating, I learned very quickly that going into a store to shop for necessities like food or clothes was not something he enjoyed doing. What did he do instead, you ask? He subscribed to subscription boxes! We cooked many Hello Fresh and Blue Apron meals together at his house. I marveled as he received boxes of clothes each month that fit him perfectly. I was intrigued with the subscription box model, and, unknowingly, he had planted a seed.

A few years later, I began tutoring math at a local after-school program. Though I had been tutoring for over 10 years, up until I started working at the after-school program, I served as a private tutor working with students one-on-one in the homes. At the afterschool program, we serve about 150 children between the ages of 8 and 18, and this was my first time working with multiple students from various schools and backgrounds at one time. Very quickly after I started tutoring there, I noticed a disturbing pattern: when my middle and high school students asked for help with geometry, algebra, or trigonometry, oftentimes it wasn't the higher-level math concepts they needed help with.

Oftentimes, it was the basics.

Fractions. Decimals. Percentages. Negative numbers. Their math foundation wasn't solid, so everything else just felt a lot more difficult than it should.

Because I am motivated by helping people feel better about math and because basic math is a life skill and a civil right, I knew I needed to solve this problem. I also knew that my solution had to be consistent and persistent, providing the regular exposure required to undo years of math anxiety and, in some cases, math trauma.

Thanks to the seed my now-husband had planted, I began studying the subscription box landscape. I learned that there were a variety of STEM (Science, Technology, Engineering and Mathematics) boxes available on the subscription e-commerce market, but none were focused on the M. As my mom says, "You can't have STEM without M!" If we want the next generation to not only engage in, but also succeed in a STEM major or career, they must have a solid foundation in mathematics. Why? Well, math is the foundation of STEM. You need math to study everything from physics to biochemistry to computer science. Even if a child does not want to go into a STEM major or career, they still need strong basic math skills in their toolkit.

At this time, I also started reading academic journals and articles about the math experiences of children, and uncovered some unsettling information about the pervasive math confidence and representation gaps in girls and children of color. I conducted customer discovery interviews with friends with daughters and my female students. As a Black woman who works with predominantly Black children, I have seen the harsh effects that limiting language and low math expectations have on Black children, especially Black girls. Armed with this research, my Bachelor of Science in Mathematics, and my years of math tutoring experience, I began working on creating a solution where a Black child, especially a Black girl, could clearly see herself as a math star. This was also going to be a solution where children of other racial and ethnic backgrounds could see a Black girl centered in a high-quality math experience, too.

That's how Black Girl MATHgic was born.

Black Girl MATHgic™ LLC (BGM) is a movement whose mission is to increase math confidence, enthusiasm, identity, fluency, agency, and persistence in children, with a focus on girls and Black children, who are disproportionately impacted by math anxiety. Our flagship product is the Black Girl MATHgic Box, which is the first and only monthly subscription box designed to increase math confidence and decrease math anxiety in girls on a third to eighth grade math level. Each box is curated with items that intentionally solve for the phenomena that contribute to low math confidence and high math anxiety, especially in girls.

ABBY BARTHOLOMEW
HBIC Smartass & Sass Box

smartassandsass.com

In late 2016, my best friend Kim and I were looking for a fun business to start together.

But before we get too far, a little history: Kim and I have been friends for over 25 years. We met in the second grade, and for the next few years we bonded over being huge nerds who loved schoolwork and the Olson twins. We started our first "business" at daycare when we were 10. We have inside jokes dating back decades, and we occasionally carry on conversations in song for no reason. We are silly weirdos who love to laugh.

So how and why did we decide to start a subscription box? Kim and I talked and texted back and forth about different business ideas. I'd been reading about the new trend of subscription boxes, and I told her about it. The recurring revenue model intrigued us. We started thinking through what our box could be. We wanted it to tick all the boxes:

- Something we were passionate about
- Something that didn't exist already
- Something people would want to get in the mail
  on a regular basis

We took a closer look at our own favorite products and discovered a common denominator—four-letter words.

We are both sarcastic souls, and had noticed a rise in vendors online who were selling sassy merch that spoke to us (because we shopped their stores regularly). After some research, we discovered that there was a huge audience of shoppers (and creators) with the same sense of humor. We found mugs, notebooks, tote bags—all kinds of brilliant sh*t that we thought we (and others like us) would love to get on a monthly basis.

And so, Smartass & Sass was born.

After our first few months in business, we discovered a surprise—sarcasm is not universal.

Everyone has their own idea of what sass means to them. For some it's all the F bombs, for others it's subtle puns. We quickly realized we needed to choose what we wanted to be (and change our messaging to reflect it).

We started surveying our subscribers, which helped us figure out some of their favorite brands and how they felt about profanity (surprise: they love it ALL!). Talking to subscribers helped us decide what we wanted to stand for, and we landed on three things:

- Supporting small businesses (and paying fair prices)
- Keeping it sassy
- Providing a variety of products (and consistently asking subscribers for their input)

Then we were able to saturate all of our materials and marketing with a more accurate brand voice, helping us keep (and find) the subscribers who were a good fit for our tribe, and saying goodbye to those who weren't.

WORKBOOK

Prompts

Your mind is probably spinning with ideas. Use these workbook prompts to outline to outline the basics of your subscription box business idea. Getting it on paper will help you gain clarity.

1. You can serve a niche best when you can clearly define it. What is the overall niche of your box? What is the community you are going to serve?

2. Next, hone in and write about your ideal target audience. This is also called your Ideal Customer Avatar (or ICA). Get as specific as possible. Instead of choosing your ICA as "moms," for example, think about a specific mom. For example, moms with young kids or US homeschooling moms. Dive deeper.

I'll get you started with some basic questions, but take it even farther than that in the space below.

- Gender:
- Age range:
- Do they have kids? If so, how many?
- Highest level of education:
- Household income:
- Occupation:
- Where do they shop?
- What hobbies do they have?
- Describe additional characteristics, traits, and habits about your ideal target. Investigate categories like their occupation and favorite restaurants. Do they frequent a gym or travel? What do they spend money on? What makes them happy?

All of these things are really important because by putting them on paper and thinking about them, you're going to get clarity in your marketing. And this will help you gain clarity about the brand in general and ultimately about what products to put in your subscription box. I promise you that this exercise will prove helpful in creating a box that really serves your audience well.

3. What will you call your subscription box? Write down the business name you decided on.

4. After researching availability, what domain name did you decide on? What's the URL where people will find you? Go ahead and purchase it to make it official.

"It's not the customer's job to solve their problem — it's yours."

— PETER GROSSMAN

CHAPTER 7
Be the Solution

Most products are born from a problem, and, more specifically, pain points that need solutions. If you have a specific problem that you are trying to solve, you are not likely alone in this search, and there are many others who will benefit from the solution you've created. Now that you've identified the key niche of your box, and, specifically, your Ideal Customer Avatar (or ICA), the next thing to do is to clearly identify the problem, or the pain points that this ICA needs solved.

Think of your box as a monthly solution to an ongoing problem. If your problem only needs to be solved one time, then it's probably not a good problem to solve with a subscription box.

But think outside the box.

Yogis. There are so many boxes for yogis! When searching for a Yoga subscription box for the purpose of this example, I came across an article titled, "The 12 Best Subscription Boxes for Yogis." Which means there are far more than twelve subscription boxes for yogis, and at least twelve appear to be doing very well. How can this be? Each of these boxes, while for the big Yoga niche, drill way down and focus on a more specific niche within that and most importantly, offer solutions to different pain points.

Some of the boxes are clothing-based, like a Stitch Fix type experience for yogis, delivering three new pieces of clothing each month for the hard-core yogi. Running out of yoga gear is likely a problem that yoga instructors, teaching multiple days a week, run into, but probably not a problem for someone who practices yoga once a week or less. Some of the boxes are lifestyle focused, and have candles and teas and other nice things that people who enjoy yoga often use in their daily lives. Others are more Buddhist-based, and are full of meditation and relaxation items. Others are primarily healthy snacks. One of my Subscription Box Bootcamp students Valeria has a yoga box that has a book club element, honing in on a specific community that enjoys yoga themed books.

The point is, as long as you are solving a problem for someone specific, there is a need for your box. People will want your box. Now let's dig into the specifics of the pain points so that you know you are solving the correct problem that will bring your audience back over and over again.

Pain Points

Marketers often talk about pain points, because one of the most effective ways to sell anything is to describe how it solves a problem for the person. It's time to get really clear about the major pain point(s) that you hope to solve with your subscription box and how you will demonstrate to your audience that your box is the solution to that problem.

One of the major pain points that we solve with Sparkle Hustle Grow revolves around training for business owners. There's a lot of clutter out there and it's often difficult to find the best online training programs and books for business and self-help. So instead of watching our customers waste precious time and energy going down this rabbit hole, we take that responsibility upon our shoulders, dig through the clutter, and curate the best of the best business training and personal development for our target audience.

Another pain point we solve is the loneliness of working from home, especially if the customer is a solopreneur. Our box provides access to a community of like-minded women business owners who can lean on each other for support, celebrate big wins, and also grow their networks through these connections. By subscribing to Sparkle Hustle Grow, our customer becomes a part of an amazing community and no longer feels alone in business.

When you're doing your market research and audience analysis, you might start to feel like the market is already saturated and that there is no room for your box. But if you get clear on your concept, be innovative, and come from a place of abundance, I have no doubt that there's enough to go around for you too!

LATONYA WILLIAMS
Founder and Chief Curator
Renew Box

www.myrenewbox.com

Sleep when you die. The grind doesn't stop. Do all the things.

I've decided to absolutely NOT subscribe to any of these popular catch phrases.

Let me tell you why.

I'm LaTonya—Wife, Mom, Jesus Girl, Daughter, Friend, Sister, Manager, Dance Mom, Social Media Consultant, Volunteer, Champion of Diversity, and Inclusion... and the list goes on! And not to toot my own horn, but I juggle all of this well. What I haven't been so good at is taking care of myself.

In early 2019, after a Christmas season of non-stop activity, I found myself easily irritated and crying over the most trivial things. Eventually I realized that I was burning out. I was so focused on doing all the things that I neglected one of the most important "things"—myself.

I started to become really intentional about self-care and I've realized that self-care is a journey, not a destination. Even though I know it's important to pause and take a moment for myself—I must admit—focusing on me has not been easy. It's a continuous process of considering my needs and taking actions to maintain my wellness.

This journey of self-care has been incredible for me and I'm still a work in progress. I know many other women have a similar story and my hope is that Renew Box will help them integrate holistic self-care into the fabric of their lives.

DEANA HICKS

Founder + Chief Inspiration Officer

One Girl Inspired

www.onegirlinspired.com

A couple of years ago, I became a full-time stay-at-home mom to a daughter who was going to be entering the world of middle school (with high school immediately following, of course) so that I could be more readily available to help her navigate what can be a complicated time in the life of a teen girl. I have loved the opportunity to be with her more, but recently started struggling with my own need for professional fulfillment; it's just the way I'm wired I guess.

After talking with many of my mom friends, I realized we are all in the same boat of attempting to ensure our teens get positive messaging as they begin to navigate the waters of their teen years. With so much negativity on social media, along with inaccurate portrayals of what teens should strive to be like on tv, in magazines, and everywhere else—I wanted to provide inspiration, empowerment, and motivation to help teen girls build confidence in themselves and be the best version of who they are as individuals so that they may grow into strong women.

As a result of all that soul searching, I started examining the things my daughter likes and purchases that bring her joy and meaning to help guide the direction of this subscription box endeavor. Right around the same time, I decided to check out Julie's Subscription Box Bootcamp after following Sparkle Hustle Grow since its launch. I decided to jump in to learn as much as I could and ramp up faster than I would have on my own. Thus, the concept was born. That was around January 2019 and my first box launched in May 2019.

LYNDSI MOORE

Founder, Cultivate Kindness Box

www.cultivatekindnessbox.com

When I was 15 years old, our community experienced a devastating loss of one of our students due to a fatal car accident. She was the 16-year-old daughter of our local church's pastor and an active member of our school clubs and programs. The day after the accident, students from every club and organization gathered at our local coffee shop where we learned of daily journals that she had kept.

In the entry written the morning of her passing, she wrote: "A community cannot be labeled as inclusive or exclusive because a community by definition is a group of people who share something in common coming together." This really made me think about the ripple of kindness that can be made through people coming together.

I launched my box a couple years ago, at 15 years old, to make a difference. We all have the ability to do so much good in the world if we just reach outside of our bubble a little bit. We can show love through kindness and acts of service for those who are hurting, lonely, sad, and lost. I want to be a generation that does something selfless for the benefit of another with no expectation of them doing anything for me. I want us to really love people. Our world is hurting right now and I want those of us here today to step up, make a difference and be known as Generation Kind!

WORKBOOK

Prompts

Just as with LaTonya, Deana and Lyndsi found, I want to encourage you that there IS room for your box, especially if you come from a place of abundance. There IS enough to go around and YOUR box is needed.

1. What are the major 1-2 pain points you hope to solve with your subscription box?

2. How will you specifically solve those pain points? What's going to delight your customers and solve that pain point month after month?

3. What will you fill the box with that supports this?

_____

_____

_____

_____

_____

_____

_____

_____

_____

_____

_____

_____

_____

_____

_____

_____

_____

_____

_____

_____

_____

_____

_____

_____

_____

_____

In the next chapter, we're going to look at the competition in your niche. I want you to remember your value proposition for the pain points you are solving and don't get discouraged if you find a lot of other similar boxes. Because your subscription box IS needed. You have the opportunity to make a box that only YOU can gift to the world.

"Companies that solely focus on competition will die. Those that focus on value creation will thrive."

— EDWARD DE BONO

CHAPTER 8

Competitive Research

One of the most important steps in the process of establishing and launching a subscription box is to look at the competitive landscape, that is, to look at the competition that's already out there. This is where a lot of aspiring subscription box business owners pump the brakes because you get so excited about your idea and then find out that someone else already beat you to it. But I'm here to tell you to shake it off, don't let it bother you. Just use it to motivate you to innovate, to be unique.

I come from an abundance mindset where I truly believe that there's enough to go around, but you still have to make your box resonate with the right people and make it something special. To stay in business, you have to bring something to the table that your competitors don't, and that unique point will attract your customers to you. For example, there's a big market for tea subscription boxes. You can discover new teas, new brands, and new flavors. There are so many options out there. How could you make your tea subscription box unique? The answer is to make it for a very specific person. Maybe you make a tea subscription box geared towards new moms with specific things included that would help her specifically in her new role, like nursing tea or relaxation tea. She sees that box and says, "Oh my gosh, that box was made just for me!" If you build a unique box concept that solves a pain point in a specific niche, it all falls into place for your potential customers.

I have competition and 100% believe that there's enough business to go around for all of us as long as we all offer a unique experience. I often think about the soda companies. There are so many different companies, but each brings unique flavors and experiences to the market. I really encourage you to have this abundance mindset. It may take some work to shift your patterns of thinking toward abundance and away from scarcity. It's so worth it! Some people like Coca-Cola, and some people prefer Pepsi, and it will be that way in the subscription box industry as well.

Competitive research is an opportunity to dive in to see who's already out there and find out what they're doing well, where they're under-delivering, and then use that information to make your own box unique and even better than the competition.

Since you've already defined your niche so clearly and know your target audience well, you should be able to determine quickly if the competitive boxes are fulfilling all of their needs and solving all of the pain points.

FINDING YOUR COMPETITORS

There are three main ways I like to find the competition and evaluate existing subscription box products in the marketplace. Just search for "subscription box" plus your niche or keywords.

- Google.com
- YouTube.com
- Cratejoy.com

If I was researching my audience for Sparkle Hustle Grow, I would look up words like *female entrepreneur, business owner, boss babe*. Are there boxes in your specific niche already? If so, how many?

And does it feel over saturated? (Remember though, come at that question from an abundance mindset. It may feel like there are too many boxes for YOU but is that really the truth when looking at it from the perspective of your specific audience?) Who are the major players that you would consider your competition?

Do this research. Go to the workbook at the end of this section and take notes on what you find before you move on to the next step. For now, write down the names of these boxes and, later, we're going to use this research to learn more from your box competition.

After you've done an initial search to see what already exists, it's time to do some detective work to make your box even better.

Look at the list that you just created of your top competition, especially the top two. Explore their websites, social media, and their Cratejoy marketplace listings (if they have one). Scroll their Facebook pages. Visit their Instagram profile. How do they present themselves on social media? What are some things you like about their branding and what are some things you don't like? Look at picture quality, engagement, content, colors, even the messages they're sending. You can evaluate this at the same time as you're building your brand. I have to note - Do not ever copy someone else's ideas or concepts or branding. Rather, you should come up with your own unique brand and your own box mission. Of course, there might be some similarities across the niche, but you still need to be uniquely you...but that doesn't mean you can't learn from the competition and what they're doing.

Here is the secret sauce: write down common themes in their customer reviews and in their comments on their social media.

A light bulb should have just turned on in your head—this is an opportunity to learn!

Comb through the online reviews of your competitors. You can learn a lot about what your target audience wants, why they come back for more, and what they loved about their boxes.

Write down the things that the subscribers loved and raved about. Then take note about the things that subscribers complained about in their reviews. Look at the one star and the two star reviews. Do you see any common complaints or common themes? Make note to avoid the things people complain about (or improve the experience) with your box.

Keep in mind, reviews can be all over the place. Sometimes they're going to be about products, sometimes they're going to be about the experience or maybe even customer service, and sometimes the review can be a rant about the postal service. All of these can potentially provide some level of useful feedback as you plan your own launch.

Next, take a look at some of their unboxing videos. You can check YouTube and Facebook for these, especially those posted by their customers. They may have some pictures of past boxes. What do you like or dislike about their products? Write it down and you might get some great ideas of potential brands to put in your box. Maybe you'll find brands or product types that you definitely do (or don't) want to put in your box. Make a note of that right now. Take some time to think about how your competition is presenting themselves and what you personally would do differently to be unique and to bring even more value than the competition does.

Take note of all of it. I bet this exercise was eye-opening, right? This exercise provides insight into what to do and what not to do, and you get to learn from your competition. It's like they're serving up the things they probably wish they knew before they launched.

As you write down these observations and ideas, you'll find actionable things to make your box even better. We continue to do this exercise from time to time at Sparkle Hustle Grow to keep our finger on the pulse of the industry and to keep us on our toes. It's important to always be innovating.

WORKBOOK

Prompts

1. Are there boxes in your niche already? How many? Does it feel oversaturated?

2. Who are the major players that would be considered your competition?

3. Visit your top competition's website, social media pages, and/or Cratejoy Marketplace listing.

4. Write down common themes in your competitors' reviews:
   - What do *subscribers* absolutely LOVE about them?
   - What do *subscribers* complain about?
   - What do *you* like/dislike about their branding?
   - What do *you* like/dislike about their product assortment?
   - What would you do differently to be unique?

_____

_____

_____

_____

_____

_____

_____

"The person who doesn't know where
his next dollar is coming from usually doesn't
know where his last dollar went."

— UNKNOWN

CHAPTER 9

How to Make a Profit

Any business owner knows that they must get a handle on their finances. You have to understand how you will make money and know where it is coming from. Before digging into subscription box business money-making tactics, let's dispel a few financial myths.

Myth 1: Subscription boxes are a get-rich-quick scheme.

I wish this was true. Like launching any other business, you need to lay a firm foundation, spend time growing your audience, and provide serious value to your customers along the way to keep them coming back for more. You also need to invest some capital upfront and should expect early overhead expenses, like the cost of your boxes, items in the box, packing materials, and shipping, along with the costs of your website and cart tools. But remember, you can use the pre-sale strategy to help with those startup costs. More on that in a later chapter.

Myth 2: You can get all of your box products for free.

This isn't true in most cases, and in fact this myth really gives our industry a bad rap. When I was at a trade show in New York City a few years ago, I saw this in action. I approached a vendor whose products we were really excited about including in our box. I introduced myself and as soon as he heard "subscription box," he said, "We don't give away free product." I was caught off guard, until I realized that he must have been asked for free stuff by subscription box owners enough times that he felt like he needed to be very clear with me up front.

Not everyone will agree with me, but here's my personal thoughts on it. First, think about the experience of getting a box of full-size items versus sample items. I know, I know, some boxes are built around the concept of providing samples but let's be honest, most aren't. A quality box that provides real value usually includes full-sized products. You can assume that most people will want full-size items in their subscription boxes and the chances of you getting amazing full size items for free at launch, are, well, pretty slim. Here's why: The people who make the product have actual hard costs to manufacture and bring a product to market, so asking them for their products for free seems a bit unrealistic in my experience. Especially if you are buying local, supporting artists, or buying other handmade items. They simply don't have room in the margin or their business model to give everything away.

Now, I have seen some vendors give samples away for free, like makeup or beauty brands, or even snack brands, but I want to discourage you from building your entire box model around the assumption that you will fill it with free items each month (unless of course you scale massively and build your platform as more of a marketing channel for vendors, but that's not likely in the startup phase). You can build a successful box and still be able to support amazing brands, without getting everything for free.

Myth 3: You will buy your products at retail stores.

NOPE! You will *never* make a profit if you buy your box items at retail stores because of their huge markups. You need to purchase wholesale so you can make a profit and build your business. You'll really hit your stride and make more money when you can capitalize on buying in bulk. It's all about the quantities of scale: the more you buy, the more you save. When you buy larger quantities of items, you'll have more negotiating power. However, this scale up to reduce overhead doesn't happen right out of the gate. It takes time to build your business, and you certainly don't want to waste precious revenue on buying massively in bulk before you need it.

Now that we've dispelled some subscription box business myths, let's move on to talking about making money!

Making money with a subscription box business model.

It's a pretty simple concept in theory. You, as the subscription box owner, charge subscribers a certain amount of money each month. You curate, buy, and ship a selection of products in the box for less than that amount. *The difference between what you charge and what it costs you is your profit.*

What you charge - Your costs = Profit

For example, say you run a bath and body subscription box.

You sell your box for $30 a month including shipping. It costs you $15 to cover the costs of products, packaging, and postage. (What I call the big three!) **Your profit is $15 per box!** In this scenario, you have a 50% margin! Ideally shoot for a 30-50% margin for your subscription box.

Now, imagine you sell **100 boxes at $15 profit each.**

100 x $15 = $1,500 in profit!

And if you sell **1,000 boxes at $15 profit each
= $15,000 in profit!**

This example is a very simplified version of how to make money with a subscription box business. There are other factors to consider in the cost of doing business like software, marketing, team members and taxes. But at least now you know the basic math of the business model!

THE ONE THING YOU HAVE TO MASTER: WHOLESALE BUYING

Wholesale buying is when you purchase items in large quantities from other companies and distributors with the purpose of reselling those items. If you are the business owner and you buy a hundred bath bombs, you're going to get a better cost by buying them wholesale than you would if you bought them in a retail store.

Introducing the concept of **"wholesale"** buying, which is when companies (or distributors) sell goods in large quantities to be resold by others.

To demonstrate the impact of wholesale buying, consider that **the typical wholesale rate is 50% off.** So if you want to include a bath bomb that retails for $5, you can usually buy it wholesale for $2.50!

To make your margins work, you need to master wholesale buying.

Using our bath bomb example, if you can buy the item for $5 at a big box store or other retail store, you're likely to get it for $2.50 wholesale. You then combine a bunch of these wholesale items for your box. You might gather $7 worth of wholesale products (perhaps, in this example, bath bomb, lotion, and soap). Then, account for packaging costs. We can use $2 as our packaging costs to cover the costs of the physical box (custom or plain with a sticker) and some filler like crinkle cut paper. Budget $6 as your shipping rate—which is low, but these items don't weigh a whole lot, so you might be able to ship them inexpensively. After adding the cost of the physical items and shipping of the box, the total is $15, thanks to wholesale purchasing.

$7 Products + $2 Packaging + $6 shipping = $15

It's pretty easy to get set up as a wholesale account for most vendors, however I'd like to share a few helpful tips to get started with wholesale buying.

Wholesale Buying Tips

In the U.S., you need to apply for a resale certificate in your state. It can sometimes be called a resellers permit, a resellers license, resale license, sales tax ID, or sales tax permit. In any case, this little guy can save you a ton of money. If you are a U.S.-based reseller, which means you're just reselling someone else's product, your resale certificate will allow you to be tax exempt when you purchase it from the wholesaler. That means you don't pay the sales tax! That can save you hundreds of dollars on product orders. Instead of you paying the sales tax when you buy it from the wholesaler, that sales tax will be gathered at your checkout if it's applicable to the end customer. Each state has its own rules about this and laws change frequently, so check out blog.taxjar. com or talk to your accountant. You will have tax settings in your ecommerce software, and, as a business owner, it's your job to understand and implement what your state requires.

When you find a product you like, check the product vendor's website. Many times they will have a link to their wholesale program and an application. If not, they might have a contact form or an email address. Email and ask them about wholesale or bulk pricing. I might make first contact through Facebook messenger, email, or even Instagram. My goal is to connect with a contact person to get the conversation started.

Many wholesalers will have a minimum buy, which can be difficult at first when you're just starting out. Usually those minimum buys are right around that $250 to $500 mark. If you aren't quite to where you can spend $250 on one product, you can get strategic and figure out how to get there. For example, maybe you look to see if they have a second product that you can buy and the combined order will be $250. Or maybe you can find a colleague, a fellow subscription box owner, or someone else that has an online store that would be willing to go in with you on a group buy.

When you're negotiating with a wholesale vendor, I encourage you to ask for a better deal. Maybe they won't give you 40-50% off out of the gate, but it can't hurt to ask for free shipping, or, "Hey, can you do any better on that price? I'm looking for 50% off." You never know unless you ask.

Pro tip: Create a media kit and show them where you're going to provide them value through marketing channels. You could offer them a chance to put a bounce back coupon in your box to drive traffic to their website, or you can feature them on your social media page. There are countless ways you can promote the company and bring them additional value by getting their product in front of your audience. I like to call it "activating the feature." First, you feature their product in your box and then you "activate" it by featuring them on social media, newsletters, and more. It's great for negotiating and getting leverage for an additional discount on your wholesale buying. In exchange for the added value, ask for a deeper wholesale discount.

In this chapter, we unpacked how to make money on a subscription box business, how you can score great product deals using the power of wholesale pricing and I gave you some of my juicy tips on becoming a pro at the wholesale game. In the next chapter, we'll cover the basics of product sourcing.

WORKBOOK

Prompts

1. Research your state's resale license needs. What is required for your state?

2. Before you buy any products in bulk, apply for a resale certificate for your state.

"As consumers, we have so much power to change the world by just being careful in what we buy."

— EMMA WATSON

CHAPTER 10

Product Sourcing

And now the big question... where do you get your products? We've learned about wholesale rates, but how do you know where the wholesalers are? And how do you score that wholesale discount?

Product sourcing is fun—it's like I get to go shopping for all of my friends—but it's also one of the most time-consuming and therefore challenging parts as a subscription box owner. A lot of thought needs to go into what items you're choosing for each month. For Sparkle Hustle Grow, I start with a theme and then I build the products around that theme. The products need to be practical, good quality, and cohesive. In addition, they need to work together from a visual standpoint to make for a great unboxing experience, and, critically, fit within the budget for each box.

Let's start with choosing the right products for your audience. Then, I'll cover where to find products.

We'll finish up with some great tips to get those products at an outstanding deal.

So, how do you choose the products?

There are five criteria, below, that provide a framework to decide if you should pursue or pass on a product.

1. **Purpose** - What purpose does each product serve and why will your target audience love it?

2. **Price** - Does each product fit in my product budget and leave room for other budget items?

3. **Value** - How do the products solve my target audience's pain point(s) or improve their life? Will they see the value in each product and in the products overall? And what is the perceived value? *Perceived Value* is the value that your subscriber perceives the product to be worth. You have to think hard about this because so often people will buy on Amazon, which oftentimes prices items at less than the retail price. And trust me when I say if you include Target dollar spot items, or items from the Dollar Store, your audience will know because they shop those places too.

4. **Size** - Do the products physically fit in your subscription box and leave room for other products?

5. **Quality** - Is the product cheap looking or is it built solidly? What is it made of? If it's plastic, for example, is it solid or is it really cheap plastic? You know what I'm talking about. You can tell when a product feels or looks cheap. You always want to get a sample in hand before buying in bulk. Many vendors will send you a free sample of the product if you ask. If not, buy one. You want to make sure that it is good quality. You want to make sure that product is up to your standards and you want that product sample so that you can place it in a box mockup to see how well it fits with the other products, both from a size perspective so that the box can actually shut, but also aesthetically. Does it look good with the other products?

Answering these questions will give you a clear answer if your product is a yes or no to include in your box.

SABRA TAYLOR-CORTESE
Founder + Gift Giving Enthusiast
The Gifter Box
thegifterbox.com

I have ADHD and I wish I had waited and gone through all the Subscription Box Bootcamp lessons and focused on my clear message instead of buying three months of products and not listening to feedback earlier. I jumped in and gave a lot of products away for feedback and started out all over the place, instead of asking for feedback before buying samples and having feedback from the actual items. I am definitely grateful for the connections and the collaborations and I have learned through trial and error, but if I had truly focused and gone step-by-step, my actual launch would have been more successful. Instead of wanting a posh little black box, I should have been true to my personality and vibrant self and created a memorable launch.

Next, where do you get your products?

This question is really two-fold: where do you find them and where do you buy them?

WHERE TO FIND PRODUCTS

I am always on the lookout for products. Whether I'm shopping online, at a local boutique, or a big box store, I have my product radar on, with my eyes open for the right fit.

When I'm out shopping, I grab samples of potential items for my box so I can experience the products myself and also mock them up in a box. If you don't have the budget, just snap pictures of potential items when you're out shopping. Those pictures can be helpful as you plan out your boxes, especially because you can poll your audience on what they'd like to receive. Post the images on social media, or send an email and ask, "Would you prefer product A or product B?" And then listen to your audience!

When I take pictures of possible items, I also take a picture of the back of the packaging, as well as price tags or labels. Remember the rule of thumb that you usually get a 50% price break when you buy wholesale. If you take a picture of a possible item that costs $5 in the store, you will probably be able to buy it at wholesale for $2.50. Having a picture of the back of the packaging is smart in case you need to know that product's item number, which is usually by the UPC code. This can help you when inquiring to the manufacturer or brand about a specific product.

PRO TIP: *You'll want to keep your ideas organized—think about adding an album in your cell phone where you keep your product ideas.*

I also have found great options for my box at specialty shops, both online and in-store retail. If you're looking for stationery, go to a stationery shop. If you're looking for party supplies, go to a party supply store. Etsy can potentially be a great place to find handmade goods that would fit in your subscription box, just keep in mind that it may be more challenging for them to offer a 50% discount.

Scout new products at retail trade shows. You can spend the day walking around with your box in hand, testing products in it to make sure they fit, introducing yourself to vendors in person, collecting catalogs, gathering samples of products, and showing vendors what it would look like to be in your box. It is a great experience and helps you build relationships and find super products in a very efficient manner.

To get started, do some research to see what type of retail trade shows would be relevant to your industry. There are vendor events for every trade: toy and baby product shows, healthy food and natural foods expos, vendor markets, etc. There are so many different events out there. We love attending the National Stationery Show. Find the events that fit your industry and take the time to go. You'll often find special deals from vendors if you order at the event. Make sure you know your numbers including how many products you need for your upcoming boxes. That way you can be ready to purchase when you've found an irresistible deal!

Once you have gathered products from stores, trade shows or have taken pictures, you can start your vendor research.

PRO TIP: Share your experience of shopping for products on social media so your audience can follow along and vote for their favorites. It creates buzz which is good for sales and retention!

I wish I had gone to a tradeshow or Atlanta market sooner in my business development so I would have had better contacts and idea development for my boxes, instead of having to research so much online on my own to find products. Going to Atlanta Market this past January helped me plan for an entire year instead of just month-to-month.

—DEANA HICKS, FOUNDER + CHIEF INSPIRATION OFFICER
One Girl Inspired
www.onegirlinspired.com

Where to Buy Products

It is tempting to get supplies through Amazon, especially in the first months of your box. In the early days, when I was shipping about 50 boxes, I did buy some products from Amazon to put into my subscription box. It made sense at the time because Amazon usually has lower-than-retail pricing, and they don't have a minimum order, which is not usually the case with wholesalers. I knew that, eventually, when I had more subscribers, I would easily be able to hit those minimum order levels to buy direct.

Another place where you can buy products for your subscription box is through distributors. A distributor is a middle-man that sits in between the vendor and the buyer. They connect buyers to brands, and many large brands use them to increase their reach without having to hire an internal team. While I don't deal with distributors frequently, there are some brands for which it's the only way to get the product. If that's the case, you'll find that out when you call the company and they redirect you to their distributor.

I get my best pricing by going directly to brands and building a relationship. Over time, you will be able to negotiate better rates and get in on closeout opportunities.

When you have landed on a product you love, first check the brand website and look for wholesale information. If you can't find their wholesale information, look for contact forms or reach out to the company via social media.

It's easier than you think to get this conversation started and obtain the name and phone number of a contact at the brand so you can speak directly to someone specifically about your box's needs. I start with a simple message:

"Hi! I run a monthly subscription box for female entrepreneurs and I'm interested in purchasing (this product) in bulk. Who can I speak to about wholesale pricing?"

That is enough to start the conversation. You want to first get the attention of the sales team and then you can provide them with details of your box, either by continuing the conversation or sending a basic media kit. You may want to indicate the quantity you'll need during these initial discussions, especially if it's a large number, because that's definitely going to get their attention. Never start the relationship by asking for free product, especially when you are brand new. This is not a good way to start a business relationship and doesn't position you as the professional that you are.

At this point in my business, I know what price ranges I can consider for products in my budget, and I share that information with vendors up front, letting them know I'm looking for products in a certain price range. Sometimes they can make suggestions on other options that are more within my budget. I make vendors aware of size limitations too. In other words, what size products will fit in my subscription boxes.

Here are additional items to keep in mind when you are talking to vendors about their products:

What is their wholesale rate for the product? Most often, 50% off retail price is a good rule of thumb but you can't assume. Ask.

How is the product packaged? Will it appeal to your audience? Will it be shipped loose packed, in boxes, in bags? Is it the same packaging as you see on their website or in store? You don't want any surprises.

Can the vendor get the product to me by my need by date? I recommend you build in 7-10 days to give a bit of a buffer for shipping delays.

Ask about product color availability. Some products will arrive in a variety of colors but if you want a specific color because it will appeal more to your audience, then have that conversation with the vendor. Again, you don't want surprises.

How heavy is the product? If you are trying to keep your box or mailer under a pound, then you need to pay more attention to this. Weight can (but not always) play a role in your shipping cost.

Is there a shipping fee? Sometimes shipping is included, but don't assume. Ask them about shipping and provide your shipping address so they can estimate shipping costs, if applicable.

At this point, you should be feeling much more confident about buying products! Making contact with brands really is a lot easier than you would think. A note that some companies may direct you to a distributor or other third-party seller and some may never even respond. It's not personal. It's just part of this business. I recommend you reach out to more vendors than you initially need. You will have future boxes to fill and it's never too early to start those business relationships with vendors you want to work with.

Before you order in bulk...

Get a sample before you make a bulk order. You want to make sure that the product is built well, is good quality, and that the packaging matches what was shown in the picture on the listing. You'll want to test the quality of the product and make sure you really love it. And, does it physically fit into your box?

Many times vendors will send you a sample free of charge, but sometimes you'll be asked to pay for it. If it's a product you really want to include, it's worth paying for the sample.

Collect all of your samples for your upcoming box and place them in a mock-up box to see how well they fit, both physically and aesthetically. If the collective appearance of the products does not make for a nice unboxing experience, don't hesitate to ask about alternate colors.

Sourcing a Box Your Customers Find Valuable

Before you buy any products for your box, it's important to understand perceived value. This is the value that your subscriber perceives the product to be worth. While we all bargain shop and find cute stuff in the Target dollar bin, if you include dollar spot items or similar, your audience won't be fooled, especially if they are Target regulars. They will know the value you're putting in is a dollar. Try to stick with items that have a higher perceived value.

You can increase your perceived value by including brand name items and aligning with reputable brands. Their reputation will boost your own. Including high quality items made of expensive-looking materials, no matter the brand, also helps.

You'll also want to think about size: if a box is packed with lots of small items, it can feel less valuable. Choose products of different sizes but if you happen to have a lot of small items, add extra filler like crinkle cut to the bottom of the box to make the unboxing experience more impressive.

In addition to the size, the weight of the items also matters. The experience of holding the box and thinking, "There's really a lot in here!" is important. Weight can impact your shipping cost, depending on the carrier you use, so it is a tradeoff between what you can afford and the potential impact on the perceived box value.

Cohesiveness of the box can also boost perceived value. Does your product variety look good together? Does it have a common theme? Themes are not a requirement but can definitely improve the perceived value because when things are coordinated around a theme or a color scheme, it looks and feels better, giving it a higher perceived value.

Finally, handwritten notes can bring a personal touch to the unboxing experience and help improve perceived value by making your brand more human. When I first launched Sparkle Hustle Grow, I included a handwritten note in my first month boxes, thanking the customer for being a founding member. Several of my customers posted these notes on social media! My customers loved the personal touch because it seems so uncommon these days. We are at the point where we can't include handwritten notes in all Sparkle Hustle Grow boxes because of the quantity, but we do reach out with handwritten notes on other occasions. For example, we send cards if a subscriber hits a certain milestone with us or to help patch up a bad experience (like a damaged or broken product.) Improving the customer experience ultimately improves the perceived value of your entire box.

Let's do an exercise to help you with your own product sourcing, based on all you've learned here. Work through this next prompt very thoroughly because this work is the starting point to a practical plan for your box!

WORKBOOK

Brainstorm a list of dream items for your box, regardless of the cost and size. This is an exercise to get it all out of your head and onto paper. Write down all the different items that you think your target audience would absolutely love to receive in their box. As you move forward with your box business, you can come back to this list as a starting point for product sourcing.

Think about:

- Solving their pain point
- Delighting them
- Finding their favorite brands

When you actually start your outreach to get product pricing, track the production information and vendor contact details in a spreadsheet.

_____

_____

_____

_____

_____

_____

_____

"Packaging can be theater,
it can create a story."

– STEVE JOBS

CHAPTER 11
Brand Packaging

Your packaging can have a big impact on your branding and your customer's experience. The experience for a subscriber begins when they receive their box at their home. What message does your box convey right away?

For the sake of talking about brand packaging, I'm going to assume you plan to ship in a box. Most subscription box businesses use "mailer" boxes, which are your traditional top-opening box with a flap for sealing. They are made with rigid cardboard, so they work well for keeping your items safe, without requiring additional packaging like wrapping them or putting them in another box. You tape them shut and slap on a label.

Now, just because you run a subscription box business doesn't mean you have to ship in a box. You could use a poly-mailer, which is more like a sealable bag. For additional protection, you can get your products packaged in something padded, like a bubble mailer. Poly-mailers are typically less expensive to customize and ship, but they are more susceptible to damage and don't provide the same unboxing experience of custom boxes.

Think about what's best for your anticipated product assortment. If you are shipping stationery, stickers or t-shirts, a poly-mailer could work. But if your product assortment varies more and needs additional protection, stick with a box.

Things to consider for packaging:

Size - The size of your box will impact your shipping. Best-case scenario, you won't change the box size each month. Think it through now so you can stick with it.

Pro Tip: Get samples of several box sizes to test out prior to ordering large quantities.

Some of the most popular subscription box sizes are:

7x5x3 inches
8x8x4 inches
9x6x3 inches
10x8x4 inches
12x9x3 inches

First, think about the size of the items you will want to ship in your boxes. What is the largest item you may include? I include a book in every box. I know that my boxes can fit a 6x9 inch book, but not larger than that. When choosing your box size, note that fragile items may need extra packaging, so build in space for that.

Second, consider how big the box should be without being too big. You want your box to feel full, not empty or simply stuffed with too much "filler" like crinkle cut. Some boxes are going to have smaller items and need less packaging.

My recommendation is to **get the smallest box that you possibly can that allows you to fulfill your mission**. Size can have a big impact on the raw costs of your boxes but also can catch you by surprise when it comes to shipping costs.

Lastly, consider postage. USPS cubic rate shipping is the one of the most popular shipping methods for subscription boxes in the US because it's cost-effective and reliable. Their cubic pricing option is based on volume and the distance of transit, not the weight of the box. In fact, it can weigh up to 20 pounds (at the time of printing this) I recommend Pirateship.com software for your USPS shipping needs.

The formula to calculate cubic rate is:

Length x Width x Height ÷ 1728 = Cubic Rate

Using this formula will determine your box's cubic tier. Your shipping rate is then calculated on a rate grid by tier and zone, (which is determined by how many miles your package is traveling.)

There is a handy calculator and rate chart on Pirateship's website so you can compare how the size of the box will impact your shipping cost. Get the link in the book companion guide at *subscriptionboxbootcamp.com/book-guide*. Why is this important? Because you can strategically size your box to decrease shipping costs.

I wish I hadn't gone with a larger box in the beginning. At launch, I thought I should order the biggest box in the shipping tier so that I could fit a variety of products inside and don't have to worry about having enough space. Sounds all well and good but the problem is that on months where your products aren't as large your box appears empty and may not convey the dollar value it actually contains. It also ends up costing more to fill with tissue and crinkle. Not to mention possibly costing more to ship.

—LEAH BRUSHETT, FOUNDER & HEAD HOT MESS MAMA
Mother Snacker
www.mothersnacker.com

Design - The design of your box can make it stand out from other mail, creating excitement for your customers when they receive it. It can also be used to support the brand and be recognizable. If you're not considering packaging as a key element, then you're missing out on one of the most effective marketing tactics for your business. The better your box looks, the more potential free marketing on social media for your box and brand. The best subscription box packaging sells itself. It creates excitement and supports your overall brand efforts.

You have two choices: custom printed boxes or plain boxes (but you can dress them up!) You may not be able to launch initially with a custom box due to costs and quantities, but you can always grow into it as you become more profitable. And that is quite alright.

If you are getting a custom box design, you may want to work with a graphic designer to get exactly what you want. We recommend Vermillion Creative, who did the Sparkle Hustle Grow box design, or 99designs, a graphic design freelancer platform. Then you provide your artwork to a custom box printer, like GivrPack, whom we admire for their social give-back component, or Company Box, another great custom box printer.

If you are buying plain colored boxes from a packaging supplier (like Uline), you will have fewer color choices but you can get really creative with how you "brand" it. I've seen some really great DIY approaches when using branded stickers or packing tape from Stickermule.

Here are a few tips to maximize your design:

- Use colors, fonts and patterns that match your brand.

- Use every side and panel if you are custom printing. It's valuable real estate for marketing. Include your logo, website URL, hashtags, or quotes that resonate with your customers. Think of strategic logo placements for photos.

- If printing on the inside is too expensive for you, know that you can always add that in a later print run. We added interior printing after four years of business. Don't break the budget to jump all in from the get go.

- Colors that pop will help it stand out from other mail.

- Lastly, box packaging is unique so this may be another great place to hire a professional designer. Some box printers have online designers but we've found better results when a designer personally creates your print.

Now that you have the lay of the land with packaging, I challenge you to decide what type and size packaging you will use and get to work on your design. This is such an exciting time for your business! Check out Pinterest to see some great subscription box packaging that may inspire your own box design.

Be sure to check out the book companion guide for all the links referenced at *subscriptionboxbootcamp.com/book-guide*.

WORKBOOK

Prompts

1. What size box will you use? Alternately, will you use a poly-mailer or bubble mailer?

2. What kind of design will you use? Custom or DIY?

3. Where will you source your boxes and/or other DIY branding elements?

"The secret of getting ahead is getting started. The secret of getting started is breaking your complex overwhelming tasks into small manageable tasks, and then starting on the first one."

— MARK TWAIN

CHAPTER 12
Operational Life Cycle

Let's talk about the day-to-day operations of your business, what I call the operational life cycle. When it comes to the subscription box model, there are several key dates that will happen month in and month out. Your operational life cycle is focused around these key dates. You need to establish these dates before launching.

We focus all of our smaller tasks around four major dates, in what we'll now call your "cycle."

1. The **sales window** is the date range when people can order your box.

2. The **cutoff date** is when any given month's sales cycle ends. For example, a customer must order before the cutoff date to get the most current box. Order after the cutoff date and the customer will receive the next box.

3. The **shipping date** is when your boxes are shipped. The shipping date should fall shortly after the cutoff date. Many subscription boxes batch ship on one specific day of the month and some have ongoing ship dates, as covered in Chapter three.

4. The **renewal date** is when your customers will be automatically charged for their next box. Depending on your setup, your renewals can all be on the same date (if you are batch shipping) or they can renew on the anniversary of their sign-up date (if you do ongoing shipping).

You've heard me mention throughout the book that I use and recommend Cratejoy. They are a pioneer and leading platform in the industry and, as such, they have expert recommendations for your cycle dates based on concrete data of what works best across many subscription boxes. Even so, keep in mind that you ultimately know your customer best. Keep their specific needs in mind when choosing your cycle dates.

Now that you know the four major operational dates of your cycle, here are my calendar recommendations:

The most intuitive and easy to communicate **sales window** is to sell from the first to the 31st. In this window, you start selling your new box on the first of each month.

BUT... think of this more as pre-selling or reserving the next month's box though. If the **cutoff date** is the 31st (or the

30th in shorter months), you want your **shipping date** to fall within four days or so of the cutoff date, let's say the fourth of the month. But if you send the *January box* on February 4th, it will confuse your customers. They will feel like it's late. In reality, you are pre-selling the *February box* all through the month of January, so you can ship the February box on February 4th. This may play out differently, of course, if you are doing ongoing (anniversary) shipping.

Why do I suggest you pick the fourth for your shipping date? It gives you a few days after your cutoff date to get your boxes prepared, labeled and dropped off at the post office.

Pro Tip: Tell your customers you ship "on or around" your ship date. That way, if your ship date falls on a Sunday when the post office may be closed, you aren't breaking any promises.

Now let's move onto your **renewal date.** With this example schedule, Cratejoy recommends that you renew your customers between the 10th and the 15th of the month. This is a timeframe in the month when consumers seem to have the most disposable income to spend on things like subscription boxes, which can help you avoid churn due to overdrafts or insufficient funds. Your customer has likely already paid their rent or mortgage and other bills. So if you sell from the first to the 31st and ship a few days later, you'll want to give at least 10 days for the box to arrive and for the customer to open it before you renew them.

WORKBOOK

Prompts

Based on the recommendations in this chapter, let's set some cycle dates. You can either use the recommended schedule which can prevent you from overthinking it. Or you can back into any of the dates—just remember to give yourself about four days after your sales cycle ends to pick your shipping date. Then give yourself another 10-15 days before you renew.

1. When will your sales cycle be?
2. When is your cut-off date?
3. When is your ship date?
4. When is your renewal date?

_____

_____

_____

_____

_____

_____

_____

_____

_____

_____

_____

"Amazing things will happen
when you listen to the consumer."

— JONATHAN MIDENHALL, CMO OF AIRBNB

CHAPTER 13
Pre-launch Steps

Up until now, you have been in the "Idea stage." You've carved out your concept and invested time to learn the basics of this amazing industry. Now for a word of caution: I know you are eager to launch and make it happen, but you shouldn't launch your box without having a proper pre-launch stage. Pre-launch is the first step toward making your box's launch a reality. I cannot emphasize enough how important this step is.

During pre-launch, you establish your business operations while building the excitement around your upcoming launch. I recommend at least two months of pre-launch so you can build your audience on the front end, while you build out your business on the backend. If you already have a captive audience, then you are ahead of the game, but you may be starting with an email list of zero. That's okay, too. You can tackle that in the pre-launch stage.

There are five steps to making your pre-launch a success. The good news is that if you've used this book and done the work as you've gone through the chapters, you should be all set for pre-launch and these five steps will feel very familiar to you.

1. Validate your concept. You've spent the time figuring out your concept and your audience, now you need to take the steps to solidify both. There's too many moving parts and if you don't have clarity of concept and audience, it won't work. Remember to keep things simple. You can use your pre-launch to test variations on your ideas and ensure you have nailed the pain point(s) you think you're trying to fix. Don't try to wing it or be that person who tries to start and launch a business on the same day, especially when it comes to product-based businesses. You need to build your logo, put some branding into your box idea, and come out the gate looking like a professional, even if you make changes along the way.

2. Grow and Nurture your email list. List-building is not to be overlooked. Growing your email list gives you an active, engaged audience for when you launch. When you have something to say, you will have someone to listen. Think about it this way, how would you feel if you showed up to deliver a really important speech, but the auditorium was empty. What?! No thank you! All that work for nothing. Start building a list of the RIGHT target audience and then connect with the people on it. Here are some of my favorite list-building tactics: giveaways, coupon codes, quizzes, and lead magnets (like a PDF download) where you ask a visitor for their email address in exchange for participating.

Build anticipation and excitement with this email list so they will be ready and willing to convert when you launch your subscription box. Even before your launch, you need to give your audience value. You need to be authentic with them and build loyalty, and prove to them that you've got something worth their financial investment. Some ways to nurture your email list include sending them updates on your progress and sharing your logo when it is finalized (especially if you asked for feedback in the process). Show them when your first set of boxes arrives. You can share product pictures, and ask them to hit reply and to vote for what they'd like to see in future boxes. It can be really simple as long as it keeps your email list engaged. Keep the conversation going so these potential founding members stay excited.

3. Build your Prototype. A prototype is simply an early sample of the box you are creating. As we covered in the product sourcing chapter, begin by going to stores, purchasing some products that you would likely include in your box and put them in a mock-up box to photograph. It doesn't have to be exactly what your first month's box actually contains, it just needs to be representative of products that might be in a box. Seeing the product assortment, the number of items, and the look of the box can jump start your marketing during pre-launch and get people excited to sign up.

4. Tech time. Even if you're not a "tech person," you are going to have to get familiar with some software to successfully run your business. You need to build your landing page to collect email addresses very early, and, eventually, you'll need to build your website so you can accept orders. You'll need a third party processor like Stripe to collect the money. To make sure your launch goes smoothly, time will need to be carved out so you can become familiar with the technology you need. Most of it is much simpler than it sounds, I promise...but tech might be an area that you outsource.

5. Pre-sale. A pre-sale is an exclusive limited-time opportunity for your email list to be the first to buy, before your box is even available to the general public. Not everyone does a pre-sale, but it was so valuable to me in launching Sparkle Hustle Grow that I had to share it with you as a vital step. Many of you, like me, will start on a very small budget and that's okay. That's what the pre-sale is for. You've nurtured your email list and built anticipation. Your ideal customers are super excited—they're basically saying, "Take my money, please!" A presale is how you do that! The pre-sale generates revenue to launch your first round of boxes. That way your first boxes are funded by money already in the bank. Also, a presale may add a little extra time to your typical sales cycle, and with that extra time, you can rack up your first sales to buy your first products. One other way to do a presale, if you have the funds already on hand to ship your first box, is to open up your first box sales to founding members—your VIPs and ONLY your VIPs—a 48 hours to week early. It creates a sense of urgency and, if you pair it with limited availability, it can positively impact sales.

I wish I knew then you don't have to start off with the best of everything. I spent thousands on professional videos, photography, a website and logo design, and marketing materials for on-site events. I was looking to establish my brand quickly and effectively, but you can build your brand one step at a time. I'm launching another subscription box in a few months and will be spending a fraction of what I did with The Happy Glamper.

—Brandi Hebert, Head Glamper
The Happy Glamper
thehappyglamper.com

STORIES
to inspire you

BETSY WILD
CEO & Founder, We Craft Box
www.wecraftbox.com

I dove in, head first! I was psyched about getting started with a subscription box business and sharing my passion for arts and crafts. I'd planned out a few things and found Cratejoy, where I could set up a fun website with a great backend, and got started.

I sent boxes to friends, a few influencers, had a handful of subscribers, and I "let'r rip!" Now, was this the best way to go about launching, maybe no, maybe yes? Little did I know at the time that this was actually my beta test, and I learned so much! After a few months of creating content, gathering feedback, and working with the Tampa Bay WaVE accelerator program in Tampa, FL., I put the whole thing on hold and went through a rebrand. I worked with an amazing marketing guru who has since become a good friend, and with his help I was able to rebrand and launch We Craft Box!

After the rebranding I was chomping at the bit to get the box out into the world and see how people would enjoy the brand new "We Craft Box!" So, as soon as I could I started selling again, but without much of a presale! Thankfully, I launched just before the holidays and had amazing traction and sales. Intuition, timing, luck, I'm still not sure, but it was a hit, and we have been thriving ever since!

LORENA HIXSON
Founder + Owner, Passion & Growth
www.passionandgrowth.com

I came up with the idea in September of 2020 after spending the day at the wineries. I immediately came home and googled how to start a subscription box. I am a subscriber of Sparkle Hustle Grow and saw where Julie had her own subscription box course. I bought the course a few days later and went through every step she had laid out.

I had no clue how to start a business. I am a full-time nurse and had never ventured into the business world or entrepreneurship. Luckily, Julie's course walked me through everything from picking the type of business to start, to opening a bank account, and eventually launching.

Needless to say I started with zero followers, no one on my email list, and no business experience. In October 2019, I created my social media pages and started collecting email addresses. I did a giveaway in order to entice people to join my mailing list. I was in the pre-launch phase for about three months. I spent this time nurturing my email list and posting content on social media. I did a presale in late December to my VIP list which only had 122 subscribers. Of those 122 people on my VIP list, 12 subscribed during the presale. I launched to the public on Jan 4th, 2020. I organically advertised on IG/FB and also did ads on both platforms. For my first month I ended with 75 subscribers, which to be honest was more than I thought. I had bought enough product for 100 subscribers so I had some boxes leftover. I listed the leftover boxes in my shop and they were sold within a week. My second month I sold out with 85 subscribers and I have continued to grow every month. It is now June and I have 350 subscribers.

JESSICA PRINCIPE

Founder, All Girls Shave Club

www.AllGirlShaveClub.com

The idea for All Girl Shave Club came to me in the shower in early 2016! I had been wanting to start a business for a while but wasn't really sure what. Then one day, I was getting ready to shave, about to steal my husband's razor for the millionth time, and the idea just came to me. "Why isn't there a shaving subscription service for women?" I envisioned a service that would not only feature a really great razor (better than my husband's!) but one that was made for me... with products that were unique and feminine and fun to use! I figured I couldn't be the only woman who felt this way about shaving and thought maybe this was something I could build a business around. I was so inspired that morning, that as soon as I finished my shower I got straight to work. I doubled down on research for about four months straight before kicking off my pre-launch.

I ran a pre-launch to test product-market fit. I wanted to make sure that women were really going to be interested in my subscription box idea before I invested money into the products, boxes, and building the brand. For me, pre-launch looked like a simple landing page with a photo of a mock-up box, as well as a short paragraph of text detailing what the subscription was and how it would benefit the customer. It had an email collector on the page so when a visitor viewed the landing page, they could leave their email address for a chance to win a free three-month subscription as well as to be notified when we launched. I also incentivized people who left their email address, to share with their friends and family. I set up a rewards system so that for every so many referrals they made, they would earn points towards other prizes and discounts at launch. This helped to organically spread the word and get my landing page in front of more of my target audience without having to spend any money upfront. I knew my idea had legs once I started to see email addresses from people I didn't know! It was really exciting! I made sure to continuously nurture my email leads throughout pre-launch. This meant staying in touch with them weekly, sending out surveys to gather their feedback and ideas, showing them sneak peeks and behind the scenes stories and photos and just staying top of mind. I still have quite a few of those original founding members with me today which I am so grateful for.

I knew from my research that about 5-10% of my email leads would convert to buying customers at launch, so I was aiming to collect around 1,000 leads. My goal was to acquire 100 subscribers in my first month after launch. Once I hit 800 email subscribers I felt pretty confident and excited to launch—I just couldn't wait any longer! My goal was 100 subscribers that first month, and I hit that within the first couple of days. I surpassed my goal of 100 subscribers the first month and continued to grow quickly that first year.

Owning my subscription box has completely changed my life. It has given me the freedom and flexibility that I craved to be able to work from home and build my schedule around my family, to serve the most amazing customers, and to earn income in fulfilling ways.

WORKBOOK
Prompts

1. I recommend that you spend a solid two to three months on your pre-launch. Keeping that in mind, when do you want to start your pre-launch phase?

2. When will you launch your subscription box?

3. If you already have an audience, start dropping hints and sharing launch information. What will you share with them to create excitement?

4. If you don't have an audience, now's the time to start building it. What list-building tactics will you use?

If you need ideas, I recommend Amy Porterfield's Online Marketing Made Easy podcast.

"Learn from the mistakes of others.
You can't live long enough
to make them all yourself."

— ELEANOR ROOSEVELT

CHAPTER 14
Common Launch Mistakes

In the fall of 2016, I ran a six week pre-launch campaign (including two weeks of pre-sale) to get Sparkle Hustle Grow into the world. I had no real training in launching a physical product, let alone a subscription box. While boxes were already popular, the training to launch one was scattered around, if it existed at all. I pieced it together as I went and figured it out. I made a lot of mistakes in those first six months. I was also very diligent in my research and spent a great deal of time choosing my vendors, and even more time trying to determine which software platforms I should use. I had analysis paralysis from the many options. The good news is that I can now save you time (and tears) by preventing you from making the same mistakes.

There are three big mistakes I see again and again when folks launch a new subscription box business. I want you to avoid them and get this right the first time around!

1. Not doing a proper pre-launch

Your pre-launch strategy can make or break you. Without this, you can waste a lot of time and money. I highly advise against deciding one day you're going to offer a box and launching it the next day. It takes time and effort to prepare for launch and quite honestly, you have to be brave and show up consistently. We talked about pre-launch steps in the last chapter, but let's review briefly.

Throughout this pre-launch stage, I was building my list, priming potential customers to buy, and getting them really excited by communicating our plans and engaging in dialogue with them. My VIP email list was invited to a pre-sale during which they received early access to the box. They had a short window to buy before I launched it to the general public. There were a limited number of boxes available for sale. Having first access added urgency as well as perceived value for my VIPs, and incentivized them even more to make the purchase.

During pre-launch, I was busy behind the scenes preparing for my upcoming launch. There are a lot of moving parts to any business, but it's particularly true for a subscription box business. It's a continuous cycle of sourcing products, selling them and packing them. Rinse and repeat. Use your pre-launch time to set up your initial systems, build your website, and get your ducks in a row. Building this foundation alongside building your list can make all the difference.

You've got to put in the work and take the time for a proper pre-launch, including building and nurturing your email list, getting your concept in front of potential early adopters (your VIPs), and creating conversations and excitement about your upcoming subscription box launch.

2. Buying items at retail price.

You're never going to make money if you buy items at retail price. Seek out great vendors and wholesalers and if you are in the US, get your reseller's license. A reminder that the general rule of thumb for wholesale buying is 50% off retail price, but that's not a guarantee. There's definitely room for negotiation and some vendors may have restrictions, but sometimes you can even get better pricing than 50% off, if you just ask for it. All of this goes into the business plan that you're developing. You definitely need to make sure you're not overspending by paying retail.

A pre-launch done well can be extremely effective! But it's also okay if you want to do things your own way. The beauty of running your own subscription box is the ability to improve and evolve every month! Learn from your subscribers, listen to what they want, tweak and adjust as you go. It doesn't have to be absolutely perfect right out of the gate (don't be too hard on yourself). We are constantly evolving and growing to be and create the best product, training, goodies, or service to delight our subscribers every month.

—BETSY WILD, CEO AND FOUNDER
We Craft Box, www.wecraftbox.com

3. Doing it alone.

I'm guilty. I did this back in October 2016 when I launched my subscription box business. I was doing it alone. I was piecing together all the parts. I was binge watching videos and I was spending countless hours doing the research. All of this was so exhausting. It took up a lot of my time—time away from my family and time away from other parts of my business like marketing and product sourcing. It made the challenge of starting a business that much more difficult. But you don't have to do it that way ...

To be honest, I never would have been able to bring Laura's Kitchen Table to life if it wasn't for Julie and the Subscription Box Bootcamp. It was the perfect guidance to walk me through every step.

—LAURA KOCKLER, FOUNDER AND CEO
Laura's Kitchen Table
www.lauraskitchentable.com

That's exactly why I created Subscription Box Bootcamp, which is an online group coaching program and community to help you grow and scale your own subscription box business. It's super supportive to have a community of people that are like-minded and going through some of the same things. I didn't have anybody to ask these questions to other than my family and I think that's one of the biggest reasons that community is so important to me now. It's critical to have a sounding board and a set of cheerleaders. It makes all the difference to have a group of people with whom you can brainstorm, lean on for support, and share your wins. I'm so grateful for the community I have now and I want that for you, too! On my own, I didn't have a roadmap. I hope you'll join me in Subscription Box Bootcamp which will provide you the tools, tech, templates and support you need as you begin your own professional journey.

Get more information at *subscriptionboxbootcamp.com*.

"You can't be that kid standing at
the top of the waterslide, overthinking it.
You have to go down the chute."

– TINA FEY

CHAPTER 15

Commit

Yay! You did it! You've made it to the last chapter! I'm so proud of all the work you've put into your subscription box so far. If you've completed all the workbook prompts, it's safe to say that you are ready to graduate from the Idea stage to the Pre-launch stage! There's still plenty of work to do before you launch your business, however, with the solid foundation you've built going through this book, you are in a great place to move forward into the next steps.

Following the system I lay out in Subscription Box Bootcamp, I was able to launch my box and grow it into a full-time income in under nine months. A large part of it was focus and strategy, but I can't deny the element of being in the right place at the right time, by intention. In month two, I went, as a vendor, to an incredible event, Christy Wright's Business Boutique. This three-day event in Nashville attracts 3000 female entrepreneurs every year. I was able to physically get in front of thousands of members of my ideal target audience to show them my subscription box, speak to them in person and build connections. The event was such a success for me—and still is! Sparkle Hustle Grow attends regularly. If you have an opportunity to be a vendor or attend a conference while you are in pre-launch (and forever after!), go for it. It can be a very successful strategy to get in front of your target audience, as it was for me. Commit to the events and actions that will move you forward.

A second game-changing event happened in month four, just as my business was finally switching from breaking even to making a small profit. I went to Dana Malstaff's Boss Mom retreat in San Diego. It was a more intimate retreat, only about a hundred women, mostly mom entrepreneurs. We were there to grow our businesses, learn from each other, and network with like-minded mamas. The smaller group was helpful, and it led to me having lots of a-ha moments. I made some changes in my business based off of the feedback I received from that event, including learning more about my target audience, changing my box price, and developing a better targeted marketing plan. And I received more validation and support—not only moral support, but tangible support too through attendees becoming subscribers!

I encourage you to get in front of not only your target audience, but also colleagues and other people who can help you in your business and support you along the way. Don't be shy about sharing and putting your concept in front of people who can provide legitimate feedback to help you improve. Stick to your plan, pivot when necessary, continue to make improvements, and commit to seeing this through.

A few final notes that I'd like to share are about comparison and mindset. It's important that you don't compare your day one to someone else's day 100. It's not apples-to-apples and it's not fair to you. It's a recipe for disaster. Instead, stay focused on building a business that is in alignment *with you, your family, and your goals.*

Also, keep in mind the idea of progress over perfection. Over the years, I learned that it's okay to make mistakes—because I sure did—and it's okay to change things along the way. This is your business so you get to call the shots.

Lastly, mindset is everything. Believe it or not, your mindset is going to be one of the biggest tools working for or against you. I encourage you to take a look at your current mindset, identify where you have room for improvement, and seek resources to help make changes that will support your wellbeing. Is it a comparison trap? Imposter Syndrome? Are you a chronic people-pleaser? For me, it was a money mindset challenge. I immersed myself in books by Denise Duffield-Thomas and Jen Sincero and made big improvements in this area of my life, which led to HUGE improvements in my business.

"Giving and receiving money is an energetic exchange between people, and your job is to consciously get your frequency in alignment with the money you desire to manifest and open yourself up to receiving it. This means getting clear on the value of the product or service you're offering, being excited and grateful instead of weird and apologetic about receiving money for it, and having total faith that this money is on its way to you instead of worrying about the possibility of its not showing up."

— JEN SINCERO, *You Are a Badass at Making Money: Master the Mindset of Wealth*

"It's okay to launch a subscription box not having done everything perfectly the first time around… and it only gets better with experience!.

—MARCELA GARCIA LANDON,
CHIEF SPARKLE PARTY MAVEN
Sparkle Party Maven party box
http://sparklepartymaven.com

SHONDA RAMSEY
Founder, Say it with Grace Box

www.sayitwithgracebox.com

For six months I sat on the idea to put together a monthly subscription box for the thoughtful gift giver—A box that includes stationery along with two giftable items for the recipient to stockpile and have on hand for those last-minute dinner invitations so they can show up with a small gift gracefully wrapped with a hand-written card to give to the host or hostess. This simple act of showing others how much you care about them is just one way we challenge the box recipients to Say it with Grace.

I sat on this idea and wondered where to even begin and then, as fate would have it, Julie Ball of Sparkle Hustle Grow was hosting a giveaway where the winner would receive many amazing tools to help launch their subscription box. On a whim, I entered, and even started to research the Subscription Box Bootcamp that was in the package. To my surprise, I won that giveaway and it was the driving force I needed to get up and get moving on this idea.

The Subscription Box Bootcamp is a tool that had exactly what I needed to confidently begin taking necessary steps in making the box a reality. Working with others like Carmen Vermillion on a logo creation and Jeremy Bower at GivrPack on the boxes gave me the confidence and branding I needed to head into a winter launch in November 2019. I'll forever be grateful for the three of them for helping me.

The experience I've had thus far with my box has been incredible. I've learned some valuable lessons and have tweaked my box a little here and there to keep meeting my subscribers' expectations. We've tried out new products, used locally sourced products, and created each box with a theme in mind.

None of this would be possible without that one day, on a whim, when I gave it a chance. **Sometimes all we need to do is make that first step in making our dreams a reality.**

FLAVIA GABRIEL
Creator, The Fabulous Planner Box
www.thefabulousplanner.com

I created The Fabulous Planner in 2015 as a hobby and it quickly blew up on Etsy. I always thought about creating a subscription box but I was terrified of the commitment and amount of work. Somehow, even with all the sales, I didn't feel confident enough to pull that off. In 2018 I decided to test the waters and I released mystery kits. I even bought cute boxes with my logo. I had only 30 and once I announced they got sold out in five hours! That was the sign I needed to invest and go deeper into the subscription business. I spent around six months learning about the business and getting my ideas together for the first six boxes. I finally decided it was time to launch and on my first month, I was sold out of boxes on the very first day. I had only 50 but still, it was a surprise to me! I was lucky to meet Julie right after I launched, I signed up to her course and learned even more! We're one year in and we keep growing every month!

Ok, Now What?

Based on the work you've done over the past 30 days, you should know by now whether you want to seriously pursue this business and if so, you have clarity around the subscription box industry and your box concept. You've already completed the Idea stage, but what's next? For many of you, this may be a huge leap of faith. Trust your gut and know you can always pivot. If you are in over your head or just don't think it's a good fit for you, that's okay. You haven't invested much more than time and heart. But if you are ready to make your box a reality, then keep reading!

So, what's it gonna be? Where do you want to be six months from now? Do you have a solid plan to get there?

Without guidance and support, it can be difficult to make any progress at all! That's why I put together Subscription Box Bootcamp for you! This is your plan to finally create the business you've imagined!

I decided to create this online group coaching program and community because I am asked daily "How do I start a successful subscription box?" **Subscription Box Bootcamp will teach you how to start and grow a profitable subscription box business… and you won't have to do it alone!**

One bootcamper shared *"I am so grateful for this community and Julie! I have worked the lessons and leaned in… taking in all the feedback and posts and it's paying off. I am so excited and absolutely loving this process!"*

Another bootcamper said *"It was by far the best investment I gave not just my business, but myself. If you are even considering launching a sub box, DO THIS COURSE! Save yourself time by shortening the learning curve, get inside knowledge, tips & tricks and access to her amazing Facebook group."*

The bootcamp core training is built in a way to help you get from Point A to Point B as quickly and easily as possible. The training covers topics from pre-launch all the way through scaling. We talk about websites, marketing, retention, systems, growing your business and so much more.

The curriculum includes over 60 lessons over the five stages of your subscription box journey. As a reminder, those five stages are Idea, Pre-launch, Launch, Systems, and Scale stages. And you already have a head start from your work in this book!

Each lesson includes short, actionable videos, demos, and resources like templates and swipe files.

Here's a breakdown of the resources included:

- Videos and software demos that walk you through the actual steps of running the business. I don't just tell you what to do, I SHOW you.

- A private Mastermind community to lean on for support, accountability and feedback as you work through the bootcamp. You'll be able to connect with fellow boot-campers, ask questions to peers who have been down your same path (at all stages of their subscription box journey), and use it as a sounding board for new ideas. My team and I are in the group frequently, meaning you'll have exclusive access to ask us questions as needed. Plus, it's a great place to sell excess inventory and find your box bestie!

- Tools and Tech so you don't waste hours and hours of research, free trials and changing your mind. I want to help make the big decisions easy. I've done the research so you don't have to. Just follow my roadmap.

- Social media templates so you can start promoting your box immediately, including post templates like spoiler alerts, a launch countdown, and theme announcements.

- Swipe files for email marketing. This includes scripts of what to say to vendors and email copy to welcome new subscribers. You simply copy, paste, and customize with your information.

- Access to our Dream Team, which is a pre-screened list of vendors we know and love in categories like graphic design, custom boxes, and Facebook ads. The Dream Team will save you hours of time researching who to hire for things you might not be able to do yourself.

- Q&A vault to help answer common questions along the way.

- Our peer-sourced vendor list will be a great place to start as you are product sourcing in different categories, saving you hours of research time.

- Resources and systems so you know your priorities each week to stay on track with sourcing, replenishing and shipping.

Go to subscriptionboxbootcamp.com to learn more—and check out the current bonuses to get you to your goals faster! On top of everything, you get LIFETIME access to all of it. That includes updates, new materials, etc.

Subscription Box Bootcamp will allow you to ramp up significantly faster than you could on your own. This is the training and roadmap you need to launch your box.

Don't just take it from me. Here's what some of my bootcampers say...

Jenn from the Mama Needs box: *"Taking this course was the only reasonable way to launch my subscription box business. I seriously don't know what I would have done without it."*

Katie from Year Cheer: *"We have launched! Thanks for all the ideas and support from Julie Ball and others in this group!"*

Valeria from Do a Shot of Yoga: *"This course is AMAZING! I had everything I needed to literally start with a vague idea, hone into something focused and strong, then build it out into a business that I LOVE working on everyday!"*

If you want a community of support to lean on, learn from and connect with, I encourage you to enroll in Subscription Box Bootcamp. We'd love to be your subscription box family!

Thank you so much for trusting me to be your guide and I hope to see you on the inside!

With gratitude,

Julie

Julie Ball
Founder, Sparkle Hustle Grow
Coach, Subscription Box Bootcamp

RESOURCES

SUBSCRIPTION BOX BASICS WITH JULIE BALL

Have a subscription box idea, but not sure where to start? Right here. Subscription Box Basics is a podcast for new and aspiring subscription box entrepreneurs. Host Julie Ball is the Founder and Chief Sparkler of Sparkle Hustle Grow, a monthly subscription box and online community for female entrepreneurs. Julie leads thousands of women through personal

development and business training in a way that's fun and supportive. She is an author, speaker, community builder, subscription box coach featured in Forbes, Business Insider, POPSUGAR, Hello Sunshine, and US Weekly. If you are ready to launch your subscription box

business idea, you need *SubscriptionBoxBootcamp.com* for the roadmap and support that will help you succeed!

Subscribe to Julie's podcast in any major podcast player or visit *www.buzzsprout.com/717357*

Get the companion guide for resources
and links mentioned in this book.

subscriptionboxbootcamp.com/book-guide

ABOUT
The Author

JULIE BALL is your Subscription Box Business Coach! She is the Founder and Chief Sparkler of Sparkle Hustle Grow, a multi-six figure subscription box and online community for female entrepreneurs. She is an author, speaker, community builder, and your business cheerleader, featured in Forbes, Business Insider, USA Today, POPSUGAR and more. She lives in the Blue Ridge mountains of western NC with her husband Kenny, daughter McKenna and mini-labradoodle, Bo.

Find her at MrsJulieBall.com

Notes

COMMIT

Notes

SPACE OF INFINITE
Possibility

Printed in Great Britain
by Amazon

38993869R00112